# The Ranger's Guide to YOSEMITE

## Insider Advice from Park Ranger Dick

by
Susan and Phil
Frank

**The Ranger's Guide to Yosemite**
1st Edition

Avalon Travel
a member of the Perseus Books Group
1700 Fourth Street
Berkeley, CA 94710, USA
atpfeedback@avalonpub.com
www.avalontravelbooks.com

Editors: Grace Fujimoto, Michelle Cadden
Graphics Coordinator: Stefano Boni
Production Coordinator: Darren Alessi
Cover Designer: Darren Alessi
Indexer: Judy Hunt

ISBN-10: 1-59880-129-5
ISBN-13: 978-1-59880-129-3
ISSN: 1941-782

Printing History
1st Edition — May 2008
5 4 3 2 1

Although every effort was made to ensure that the information was correct at the time of
going to press, the author and publisher do not assume and hereby disclaim any liability to
any party for any loss or damage caused by errors, omissions, or any potential travel disrup-
tion due to labor or financial difficulty, whether such errors or omissions result from negli-
gence, accident, or any other cause.

# Contents

# Acknowledgments

We wish to thank Josh Englander for his invaluable help in developing and editing the initial manuscript; Stacy Frank for her help in carefully revising and updating the manuscript; Frank Ansley for revising the illustrations; Doug Davis for his work on a web and telephone directory for the new edition; Keith Walklet of Yosemite Concession Services Corporation for his ongoing advice and support; Steven P. Medley, Beth Pratt, and the Yosemite Association for their generous assistance with research and resource materials; Kenny Karst of Delaware North Parks and Resorts at Yosemite; Annie Malley of the Bio-diversity Resource Center, California Academy of Sciences, for her technical expertise; the National Park Service staff at Yosemite, especially Dean Shenk for his careful review of the manuscript; and Bruce Brossman, Christine Cowles, Norma Craig, Linda Eade, Scott Gediman, Adrienne Freeman, Oly Olsen, Kendell Thompson, and Steve Thompson for their technical assistance and help in making this guidebook as accurate as possible. We would also like to thank Grace Fujimoto of Avalon Travel for her invaluable help in making this new edition possible.

S. F. and P. F.

This book is dedicated to the memory of Philip N. Frank and
Steven P. Medley...irreplaceable voices of Yosemite.

## Introduction

Hi, my name is Ranger Dick Ewart, and I'll be your guide through this handbook. I arrived in Yosemite in the fall of 1975. As with most first-time visitors, I was overwhelmed with the beauty and majesty of the park. Trying to understand the magnificence of this place left me a little bewildered. I wanted to learn more. How do those trees grow directly out of a bare rock face? Where do the waterfalls come from? How did Yosemite Valley form? I had lots of questions that needed answers. So, I spent my first afternoon taking a naturalist walk with Ranger Roger McGehee. By the end of the hike, I not only had all of my questions answered, but I had made up my mind that I wanted to become a ranger so I could interpret the natural history of this spectacular place for visitors like me.

Over the past 30 years, I've been able to answer for countless visitors those very same questions that I had that first day as I stood in awe in Yosemite Valley. What I have learned as a ranger at Yosemite National Park is that the more you experience and explore this amazing place, the more you want to learn. If you have never been to Yosemite, this feeling of awe awaits you. If you are returning after multiple visits, you already know the feeling and have undoubtedly developed your own connection with this special place.

May this Ranger's Guide help to answer your questions before and during your visit to Yosemite. Carry it with you. But save a few questions for me, and come on a ranger-guided hike. I look forward to your visit.

**Ranger Dick Ewart**
**Yosemite National Park**

## Author's Note

The question-and-answer format of this book originally came from "100+ Common Visitor Questions & Answers," a document that the National Park Service's Division of Interpretation at Yosemite National Park prepared and revised in April 1995 to help park rangers and interpretive staff at Yosemite get quickly oriented.

Working from that idea, we have put together many of those same questions plus lots of others to help visitors get quickly oriented. We hope the book will add to your enjoyment of this beautiful park.

# I.
# Getting there

# Where **is** Yosemite?

**O**n the eastern side of California, where mountains reach the sky and trees outnumber people, Yosemite sits atop the Sierra Nevada, spilling down both sides of the range to about 30 miles from the Nevada border and 225 miles from the Pacific Ocean. We're closer to Oregon than Mexico, so if you imagined California as a bear standing up, we're about at its left elbow.

Here are some road mileage figures and approximate driving times to Yosemite Valley to help you plan your trip (based on 50 mph outside the park and 35 mph inside the park):

## Via Highway 41

- From Los Angeles — 313 miles (6.25 hours)
- From Bakersfield — 201 miles (4.25 hours)
- From Fresno — 94 miles (2.5 hours)
- From Oakhurst — 50 miles (1.5 hours)
- From Fish Camp — 37 miles (1 hour)

## Via Highway 140

- From San Francisco — 219 miles (4.5 hours)
- From Sacramento — 199 miles (4 hours)
- From Stockton — 140 miles (3.5 hours)
- From Merced — 81 miles (2 hours)

- From Mariposa       43 miles (1.25 hours)
- From El Portal      14 miles (30 minutes)

## Via Highway 120 from the west

- From San Francisco  195 miles (4.5 hours)
- From Sacramento    176 miles (4 hours)
- From Stockton      127 miles (3 hours)
- From Manteca      117 miles (2.75 hours)
- From Oakdale       96 miles (2.25 hours)
- From Sonora        60 miles (2 hours)
- From Groveland     49 miles (1.5 hours)

## Via Highway 120 from the east

- From Las Vegas      460 miles (8 hours)
- From Los Angeles   409 miles (9 hours)
- From Reno          218 miles (5 hours)
- From Lake Tahoe    190 miles (4.5 hours)
- From Carson City   188 miles (4.5 hours)
- From Bishop       146 miles (3.5 hours)
- From Mammoth Lakes 106 miles (2.5 hours)
- From Lee Vining    74 miles (2 hours)

## How do we get there?

**D**epending on time and money, you can get to Yosemite Valley by car, bus, train, or plane.

Drivers have a choice of four roads to the park. From the south, Highway 41 runs from Fresno through Oakhurst and Fish Camp to the South Entrance, where you'll find the Mariposa Grove of giant sequoias and the Wawona Hotel (1.5 hours from Fresno).

From the west, Highway 140 rolls along the river through Merced, Cathey's Valley, Mariposa, and El Portal to the famous Arch Entrance (approximately two hours from Merced). From here, it's an easy uphill drive along the river into the valley.

Highway 120 from the northwest wanders through Manteca, Oakdale, Moccasin, Groveland, and Buck Meadows, winding up at the Big Oak Flat Entrance (a little less than two hours from Manteca). This steep descent into the valley provides spectacular vistas.

Starting from the east, your only access is through Lee Vining near Mono Lake and over California's highest auto route: the 9,945-foot Tioga Pass, which leads into the park's high country wilderness (close to 2.5 hours from Lee Vining). This section is always closed in winter. For recorded road and weather information, contact General Park Information for Yosemite National Park (209/372-0200, www.nps.gov/yose/planyourvisit/conditions.htm).

Of the hundreds of bus companies that come to Yosemite, I'll mention just a few to give you an idea of the range of services available. VIA Adventures (800/VIA-LINE, 209/384-1315, www.via-adventures.com) offers a Yosemite-in-a-Day tour, which includes transportation, water, a boxed lunch, and a two-hour Yosemite Valley tram tour.

From Northern California, one-day bus excursions with Tower Tours (866/345-8687, www.towertours.com) or Gray Line (888/428-6917, www.grayline.com), depart from San Francisco. For a little more luxury, California Parlor Car of San Francisco (415/474-7500, www.calpartours.com) offers one-, two-, or three-day tours with overnight stays at the Yosemite Lodge or

Ahwahnee Hotel, one lunch, and a two-hour valley tram tour. Or, for a bus of your very own, call Preferred Charters (707/585-9110) in Santa Rosa.

With daily AMTRAK (800/872-7245, www.amtrak.com) train service from Oakland/Emeryville to Merced, and from Los Angeles and San Diego to Fresno and Merced, you can ride some of the way by rail and the rest by bus. AMTRAK handles the VIA bus connection into the park. YARTS (877/989-2787, www.yarts.com, phone hours Mon.–Fri. 7 A.M.–6 P.M.) is a good resource to learn about bus schedules, the Merced airport, or Merced Amtrak station.

Birds can land anywhere in Yosemite, but you'll have to fly into one of the San Francisco Bay Area airports (San Francisco, Oakland, or San Jose) and drive 4.5 hours to the park, or into one of the Southern California airports (Los Angeles, Orange County, Burbank, or Ontario) and drive 5.5 hours to the South Entrance. Closer to the park, you can take one of 14 airlines to the Reno-Tahoe Airport, then drive three hours to the Tioga Pass Entrance. Landing in Fresno or Merced, you can drive 1.5 hours to the South Entrance or catch a YARTS bus from the Merced airport. Call the airlines or a travel agent for more information.

# What's the best time of the year to see Yosemite?

**E**very season in Yosemite has something special to offer. The blooming of spring is one of my favorite times, when fresh colors and the calls of wildlife emerge from the big freeze. Runoff from snowfall swells the rivers and creeks, giving visitors a thunderous display of our famous waterfalls. Best of all, there are fewer visitors in March and April, which means less of a crowd at the exhibits, restaurants, and stores. Since the park is still digging out from winter, some of our campgrounds and trails are not yet open, especially in the high country.

Summer (June–Labor Day) is the season of more: more people, more activities, more campgrounds to choose from, and more services available. Most of the waterfalls dry up, but the rivers and lakes have better fishing. Backpackers, wilderness campers, and rock climbers love using the long, warm days of the season to tackle Yosemite's challenging landscape.

The fall (Sept.–Nov.) leaves us with good weather, fewer people, and a chance to experience the slow withdrawal of nature into winter. However, there's less daylight in which to see the colors of the trees and fields, which are glowing with the brightest colors of the year.

Winter's sleepy spell transforms the park into another world. It's time for visitors to trade in their hiking boots for skis and snowshoes, and experience Yosemite at its most serene. Some access roads close, but many of the park's facilities remain open, including four of the campgrounds: Upper Pines and Camp 4 in the valley, as well as Hodgdon Meadow and Wawona.

Hmm...

It's certainly cheaper than an amusement park, where the mountains are fake and the animals are usually people in costumes. As you enter one of the four park gates, you'll pay an entrance fee that's good for seven days, and the ranger will give you a copy of the Yosemite Guide with basic park information and a copy of the *Yosemite Today,* the park newspaper with up-to-date listings about guided programs and park activities. Hours of operation for visitor centers and the commercial realm are available as well. Want to do some advance reading? To see recent issues of the paper visit: www.nps.gov/yose/planyourvisit/today.htm. For educational fee waivers, contact the Yosemite Fee Office (209/372-0207, www.nps.gov/yose/planyourvisit/waivers.htm).

**Private non-commercial vehicles**..................................$20
    *(valid for seven days)*
**Individuals arriving by non-commercial bus, foot, bicycle, or horse** $10
    *(valid for seven days, free to those 15 years old or younger)*
**Individuals arriving on motorcycle**............................$10
**Annual Yosemite Pass**...........................................$40
**America the Beautiful Annual Pass** .............................$80
    *(good for all National Parks and Federal Recreation Lands for one year*
    *from date of purchase—this pass replaces the National Parks Pass and*
    *Golden Eagle Pass)*
**Senior Pass** ....................................................$10
    *(lifetime admission and discount pass for all National Parks for U.S. citi-*
    *zens or permanent residents who are 62 and older)*
**Golden Access Pass** .......................................... Free
    *(lifetime admission and discount pass for blind or*
    *permanently disabled U.S. citizens or permanent residents)*

## Is the park always open to visitors?

The park is supposed to be open 24 hours a day, 365 days a year, but every once in a while Mother Nature decides to temporarily close the gates.

In 1997, starting on January 1, two and a half days of warm and heavy rains brought the greatest flooding to hit Yosemite Valley in 100 years. The flooding closed the valley completely for two and a half months. The rough winter runoff of 1995 created a heap of problems in spring and summer. In March, flooding and rock slides caused by winter runoff closed two main entrances and the high country trails; a couple of months later, we had a June snowstorm that dumped so much snow that the High Sierra Camps and roads outside Yosemite Valley had to be closed. In 1990, lightning storms started a series of fires that shut down the entire park for a week. For current 24-hour information on park and road conditions, contact the National Park Service (209/372-0200, press 1, then 1 again; www.nps.gov/yose/planyourvisit/conditions.htm.)

It's not always Mother Nature's fault; sometimes it's just plain human nature that makes the park inaccessible. In 1995, there were so many visitors motoring around the park that it became impossible for anyone to drive into Yosemite Valley—seven weekends in a row!

For the first time in the park's history, Yosemite was closed to visitors twice in 1995 because of a government shutdown. During the Christmas season, all the hotels and visitor facilities were empty.

The park is open 365 days a year!

Nature permitting...

# Facts About Yosemite National Park

- Native Americans lived in Yosemite 4,000 years before the Gold Rush.
- First tourists arrived in Yosemite in 1855.
- John Muir first visited Yosemite in 1868.
- Yosemite National Park was established on October 1, 1890.
- David and Jenny Curry opened a small camp for tourists in Yosemite in 1899.
- The size of Yosemite is 748,542 acres, or 1,169 square miles.
- 94 percent of the park is designated wilderness.
- Yosemite has:

    360 miles of paved roads

    800 miles of developed trails

    880 miles of rivers and streams
- Yosemite Valley is seven square miles.
- 75 to 80 percent of all visitors to Yosemite stay in the valley.
- Growth in Annual Visitors to Yosemite:

    | Year | Visitors |
    |------|----------|
    | 1855: | 42 |
    | 1899: | 4,500 |
    | 1922: | 100,506 |
    | 1940: | 506,781 |
    | 1954: | 1,008,031 |
    | 1986: | 2,982,758 |
    | 1991: | 3,547,163 |
    | 1996: | 4,190,557 |
    | 2006: | 3,242,644 |

# What services are available?

**M**ost of the visitor facilities and services are in Yosemite Valley. That's probably why 75–80 percent of park visitors spend all their time in the valley. Here's what you'll find within its seven square miles: the Visitor Center, Ahwahnee Hotel, Yosemite Lodge, Curry Village, Ansel Adams Gallery, Housekeeping Camp, a grocery store, deli, post office, repair garage, free shuttle service, medical clinic, a wilderness center, chapel, bicycle rentals, recycling center, campgrounds, ATM machine, cashier's office, public restrooms, showers, laundromat, a jail, and photocopy and fax machines in the hotels. Ah, yes—the great outdoors.

About 25 miles south of Yosemite is the historic community of Wawona. Here you'll find the Wawona Hotel, Pioneer Yosemite History Center, a grocery store, gas station, and nine-hole golf course. There's no shuttle or regular commercial bus service to this part of the park.

Most of Yosemite National Park lies 55 miles north of the valley; a good chunk of this portion is wilderness area. Most of the services in this part of the park can be found in and around Tuolumne Meadows, including the Visitor Center, four lodges (two lodges inside the park and two just outside its boundaries), two gas stations (Tuolumne Meadows and Crane Flat), a store and grill, post office, ranger station, wilderness permit station, restrooms, and countless miles of the best trails in the Sierra Nevada.

Hi. We're most, hungry, need an ATM, a bathroom, gasoline, a room and we want to mail this postcard.

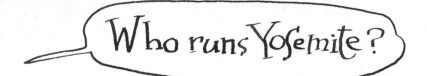

# Who runs Yosemite?

The United States National Park Service (NPS), which is part of the Department of the Interior, makes the rules in Yosemite National Park. This means you won't see any highway patrol, sheriffs, or municipal firefighters during your visit.

The NPS has plenty of people around who make sure things run smoothly. Rangers handle law enforcement, traffic regulation, search and rescue, and other duties. Interpretive rangers provide all the educational walks, talks, and programs in the park. The people dressed in green pants, gray shirts, and dark green baseball caps are the park maintenance, fire, and resource management workers. All of these people answer to the NPS administrators, such as the superintendent and chief ranger, who manage Yosemite from their park offices.

To help with all the lodging, food services, bus tours, horse rides, and most of the shops in the park, the NPS has a contract with a private concession company, but the NPS authorizes the prices and service rates. The Yosemite Park & Curry Company had the job for 70 years, until 1993, when the Yosemite Concession Services Corporation (YCS) took over with a 15-year contract. YCS later changed its name to DNC Parks & Resorts at Yosemite.

**You can contact the NPS and DNC Parks & Resorts at the following addresses:**
National Park Service
P.O. Box 577, Yosemite National Park, CA 95389
209/372-0200 (General park information; recorded)
800/436-7275 (Camping reservations)
www.nps.gov/yose

DNC Parks & Resorts at Yosemite, Inc.
P.O. Box 578, Yosemite National Park, CA 95389
559/253-5636 (Accommodation reservations)
www.yosemitepark.com

# Where can we stay?

There are close to 1,500 rooms within the park, ranging from basic to deluxe. To get the best place for your needs, reserve early. Reservations for most lodgings are made through the DNC Parks & Resorts at Yosemite, Inc. (559/253-5636, www.yosemitepark.com/Reservations.aspx)

If you want to stay in the valley, you had better reserve your lodging as far in advance as possible, which is one year and one day (366 days) before your arrival. This way, you'll probably get your first choice of rooms in Curry Village, Housekeeping Camp, Yosemite Lodge, and the Ahwahnee Hotel. The same goes for other lodgings in the park, including the Wawona Hotel, White Wolf, and the Tuolumne Meadows Lodge in the summer.

The rates vary according to amenities offered. A basic tent cabin with cots, blankets, and a bathroom nearby costs $76 per night, while a billowy bed at the Ahwahnee Hotel runs over $400 per night (rates subject to change).

You can also bunk down at a place outside the park, where various lodges, hotels, and motels await. For more information, turn to the *Lodging and Dining* and *Camping and Backpacking* chapters.

# What should we bring?

**I** suppose you could bring just about anything, like a bowling ball or a lawn-mower, but they're not going to do you much good here. What you should bring depends on your accommodations and activities of choice, but I can tell you some basic items that will make your trip more comfortable. For advice on special activities, turn to the corresponding sections of this book.

Our weather is generally predictable. We have warm days and cool nights (spring–fall), so remember to bring an extra layer of clothing for evenings. In the winter, our temperatures average in the high 40s and 50s in the valley, but the higher you go, the colder the air. A cotton sweatshirt and a pair of jeans won't be enough, but a wool sweater underneath a water-resistant shell will work. Heat escapes from your head and hands, so pack a pair of gloves and a cap that covers your ears.

I've seen people in the park who are red as a radish and covered with bug bites, but you can save yourself the misery by bringing sunscreen and insect repellent. A first-aid kit is always a good idea, along with a pair of boots or sturdy sneakers for hiking, walking, and bicycling. Binoculars will help in spotting wildlife, and a camera will provide the proof that you were here. Once you're tucked away in your tent or cabin, it's always nice to have a good book and games to while the night away.

# Can Fido come, too?

Y ou can bring your pets with you as long as you follow some strict rules. Pets must be leashed at all times and are only allowed on paved roads and bike paths. They can't follow you on trails, in buildings, or in the backcountry, unless they're service/assistance dogs for people with disabilities.

We do have "pet camping areas." In the summer, you and your furry friends can pitch a tent at Upper Pines, Wawona, Bridalveil Creek, Hodgdon Meadow, Crane Flat, White Wolf, Yosemite Creek, and Tuolumne Meadows. In the winter, pets are allowed in three campgrounds: Upper Pines, Wawona, and Hodgdon Meadow.

These rules are made for good reason. Our delicate ecosystem isn't ready for the wild mountain Chihuahua or free-range Labrador. Just about any kind of pet could create problems for the park wildlife and their natural habitats, not to mention other visitors.

A 10-stall, open-air kennel is maintained at the Yosemite Valley Stables in summer. Dogs weighing more than 10 pounds can be boarded here. For more information, please call 209/372-8348. You can check with the following boarding/kennel facilities for your pet: Graydon Kennels (Oakhurst, 555/683-8836), Hoof N Paw (Oakhurst, 555/683-3313), Ritter Animal Hospital (Mariposa, 209/966-5666), The Animal Care Center (Mariposa, 209/742-7387), and Doggone Gorgeous (day boarding only, Groveland, 209/962-4688).

# Record-Setting Geology

- El Capitan (3,000 feet) is the tallest unbroken cliff in the world. The first climb of El Capitan's face was made in 1958.
- Yosemite Falls (over 2,400 feet) is the highest free-falling waterfall in the United States, with Sentinel Fall (2,000 feet) a close second.
- High water measurements in Yosemite Valley:

  | 23.45 ft. | January 2, 1997 |
  |-----------|-----------------|
  | 21.52 ft. | December 23, 1955 |
  | 16.96 ft. | December 23, 1964 |

- Yosemite's 10 highest peaks:

  | 1. Mt. Lyell: | 13,114 ft. |
  |---------------|------------|
  | 2. Mt. Dana: | 13,053 ft. |
  | 3. Rodgers Peak: | 12,978 ft. |
  | 4. Mt. Maclure: | 12,960 ft. |
  | 5. Mt. Gibbs: | 12,764 ft. |
  | 6. Mt. Conness: | 12,590 ft. |
  | 7. Mt. Florence: | 12,561 ft. |
  | 8. Simmons Peak: | 12,503 ft. |
  | 9. Excelsior Mountain: | 12,446 ft. |
  | 10. Electra Peak: | 12,442 ft. |

# II

# Park Attractions

We only have a day to visit. What should we see and do?

When long-time ranger Carl Sharsmith was asked this question, he replied, "Go out into that meadow, sit down, and cry." Well, I'd like to offer a few more suggestions. For starters, leave your car (follow signs to day-use parking at Curry Village) and take the shuttle bus around Yosemite Valley. The Valley Visitor Center will give you some good background information, then you can hike around the valley and see the real thing.

Other one-day visitors might like to take a two-hour tram tour of the valley's famous sites—adult rate is $22, child rate (five and older) is $11.50. The tour leaves several times daily from shuttle stop #8—Yosemite Lodge at the Falls. Be sure to check out your copy of the *Yosemite Today* for exact departure times. This tram operates year round with an open-air vehicle in the summer and a heated tram in the winter. Call 209/372-1240 to make reservations prior to your arrival at Yosemite.

You might also enjoy the one hour and fifteen minute Big Trees Tram Tour to see the Mariposa Grove of the Giant Sequoias. The tram tour departs daily 10 A.M.–5 P.M. in the summer and costs $16 for adults and $11 for children. Call 209/372-4386 to purchase tickets.

## SOME SURE-FIRE STOPS:

### Yosemite Valley Visitor Center
Located in the Yosemite Village, the center offers ranger-led tours and a video tailor-made for you one-dayers called *One Day in Yosemite*.

### Yosemite Museum
Next to the visitor center, the museum offers changing displays of famous Yosemite artwork. There's also a re-created Miwok Indian village, where you can take a self-guided walking tour.

## Walk to Lower Yosemite Fall

From shuttle bus stop #7, you can walk a quarter mile to the base of Lower Yosemite Fall, one of our greatest sights (30-minute walk).

## Happy Isles Family Nature Center

Near shuttle stop #16 (summer only), the Nature Center has films, exhibits, and nature programs for kids during the summer. From here, you can walk less than a mile to Vernal Fall Bridge for the best view of the fall. If you have energy to burn, hike on along famous Mist Trail to the top of Vernal and Nevada Falls (8.5 miles).

## Walk to Mirror Lake

It's a half-mile to Mirror Lake from shuttle stop #17. The lake is filling with sediment, but it still has an awesome view of Half Dome. If you find a meadow instead of a lake, that means it's already completed its yearly late-fall transformation.

## Mariposa Grove of the Big Trees

Yosemite's largest grove of giant sequoias is located near the South Entrance on Highway 41. During the summer, trams take you through the grove for a fee, or you can take the steep hike to the top. The grove's museum exhibits a natural history of the trees, including the amazing Grizzly Giant and the fallen Tunnel Tree (open summer only).

## Spectacular Views of Yosemite

Just one hour's drive from the valley, Glacier Point offers a bird's eye view of the entire valley. Exhibits describe the geology of the park and identify major peaks (Glacier Point Road is closed in winter).

From the valley, follow road signs to Highway 41 toward Fresno, then turn left into the Bridalveil Fall parking lot, a 15 minute drive from the eastern end of Yosemite Valley. A short trail leads to the base of the fall, where water plunges 620 feet to the valley floor

Also from Highway 41, drive approximately one mile to the Tunnel View turnout. This is the historic panorama seen by Yosemite's first non-native visitors over 150 years ago (10–15 minute drive from the eastern end of Yosemite Valley).

Open in the summer only, the Tioga Road takes you through magical Tuolumne Meadows. Don't miss Olmstead Point looking out over Tenaya Lake and the back side of Half Dome.

**G**etting a feel for the park is like eating a scoop of ice cream: No matter which flavor you pick, it's going to be good. I suggest leaving your car at the Curry Village day-use parking lot and taking a free year-round shuttle around Yosemite Valley, the heart of the park. In the summer, you can ride the El Capitan shuttle that stops at "El Cap," Four-Mile trailhead, and the Valley Visitor Center. You can also ride the Tuolumne Meadows shuttle between the Tioga Pass and Olmsted Point. In winter, a shuttle bus will take you to Badger Pass twice daily.

The Yosemite Valley Visitor Center (shuttle stops #5 or #9) is a great place to get your bearings. You can talk to rangers, view the Yosemite slide show and videos, browse the bookstore, and pick up a copy of the *Yosemite Today* newspaper for the latest information on park activities and operating hours for the shops, museums, and rental sites.

From there on it's up to you. You can ride the free shuttle to one or all of the 22 stops along the route (buses run every 15–30 minutes, 7 A.M.–10 P.M.), or take a two-hour tram tour of all the valley's famous sights and learn about the park's geology, history, and wildlife from the guides. Stop by any of the tour and activity desks to purchase tickets. For families, another choice is the *Road Guide*, available at the visitor center. It guides you to hundreds of sites in the park, describing the park's scenery, geology, and history along the way.

Hikers and backpackers won't want to miss the Wilderness Center, just east of the Visitor Center on the pedestrian mall. There's plenty of information on the park's backcountry, complete with educational exhibits and a helpful trip-planning section. This is also the place to get your free wilderness permits or make camping reservations up to 24 weeks in advance.

# How was the Valley formed?

**W**ould you believe the entire park was once beneath the sea? That's when the story begins, about 470 million years ago.

Due to a number of geologic processes—including the shifting of the earth's tectonic plates—and moisture and heat deep under the ocean floor, rock melted and the Sierra Nevada mountain range began to rise about 100 million years ago.

The molten masses cooled to granite rock, leaving a broad valley of rolling hills with a river now known as the Merced River running through it. Meanwhile, further uplift carved into the river and hills, cutting into the once-broad valley, beginning its transformation into a steep canyon rimmed by granite peaks.

More than one million years ago, nature got its own Michelangelo—the Ice Age. Ice filled the entire region, and like a sculptor chiseling away at a huge block of marble, the ice began carving the land into what it is today: steep cliffs, rounded domes, and a lush valley floor. When the last glaciers melted away 20,000 years ago, they left behind a lake in the valley. Today you can roam around the forests and meadows that have taken its place.

## Broad Valley Stage

About 25 million years ago, Yosemite Valley was a rolling landscape of low hills and a broad valley with the Merced River meandering through it. El Capitan rose in gentle curves to a height of only 900 feet, and Half Dome could be seen as an irregular form 500 feet above the lay of the land. There were no dramatic cliffs or waterfalls.

## Canyon Stage

From 10–2 million years ago, great uplifts and large water runoffs caused the Merced River to cut into the valley floor, forging a deep, walled canyon with a fast-moving river. The Yosemite uplands area rose several thousand feet above the river but had not yet acquired the sharp-edged rims that we see today.

## Glacial Stage

More than one million years ago the Ice Age brought glaciers from the High Sierra down through Yosemite Valley, widening its river canyon, steepening its walls and rims, and polishing its domes and towers. As the last glacier left, it cut back the rough walls of the deep river canyon, widening the valley and revealing sheer, smooth cliffs and its spectacular waterfalls.

## Lake Stage

After each glacier, the floor of the valley was covered by a lake. The last glacier left ancient Lake Yosemite, which was probably up to 2,000 feet deep. Since then the lake basin has filled with earth, and in its place are the meadows and forests that park visitors enjoy today.

## What happened to the other half of Half Dome?

**S**ome people see our famous landmark as half empty, others think of it as half full. I just see it as a big rock reaching to the sky.

It seems I might be closest to the truth. According to geologists, it never was a complete dome. Millions of years have chipped away just a small portion of the granite mountain. The latest guess is that only 20 percent of Half Dome's size has been worn away over the ages.

So where did that portion go? During the Ice Age, more than one million years ago, glaciers filled nearly the entire valley, leaving only the top 700 hundred feet of Half Dome's 4,800-foot height above ice. The melting glaciers likely washed away small portions of Half Dome to the valley floor, leaving them buried in the earth. Other pieces may have been swept away by flood waters to places as far away as the San Joaquin Valley.

Over time, Half Dome will probably continue to be whittled by the same forces and carried to faraway places, including the Pacific Ocean.

See dotted line!

# What's the best way to see the waterfalls?

**A**lthough we have 13 falls in the park, only four are accessible by trail. During spring's snowmelt, the waterfalls come crashing down, until summer, when most of these great rushes have slowed to a trickle or have completely dried up. If you're a waterfall hunter, the best month to catch your prey is usually May.

## Yosemite Falls

Upper and Lower Yosemite Falls, with a cascade between them, add up to be the highest waterfall in North America, over 2,400 feet. One of the best views of this year-round waterfall is seen in spring. Looking up from the valley as the early afternoon sun casts shadows on the falls, you'll see jets of water shoot out clearly from the granite cliffs.

There are a few ways to get to the Yosemite Falls trailhead. You can take the shuttle from the Valley Visitor Center to stop #7 at the Yosemite Falls parking area and walk 10 minutes to the base of the falls. You can also walk down the bicycle path from the Visitor Center. Following the "Park Exits" signs by car is an option, but in the summer you'll need some luck finding a parking space.

## Bridalveil Fall

Plummeting 620 feet down the west end of the valley, Bridalveil Fall is famous for its veil of mist, best seen around 1 P.M., when it's lit by direct sunlight. Bridalveil is another of our all-season falls, dropping from a "hanging valley" just behind the cliff top.

Off Highway 41 toward Fresno, the Bridalveil parking lot is the start of a 15-minute walk to the base of the falls. Don't forget: from Yosemite Valley there are two signed turns for Highway 41, and you must take them both.

Lower Yosemite Fall →

## Vernal and Nevada Falls

Flowing down Yosemite's "Giant Staircase," the Merced River takes two big drops down to the valley below: Vernal Fall's 317-foot drop and Nevada Fall's 594-foot giant plunge.

The view of Vernal Fall from Happy Isles, which the Miwok called the "Meeting of the Waters," is best seen in the morning. If you walk up the trail from the Nature Center around 10 A.M., you just might see the sunlight transform the plunging water into falling jewels. Nevada Fall usually comes to life later in the morning, when the light casts curious shadows on the cliff face.

To get there in the summer, take the shuttle to stop #16 at Happy Isles, where signs will guide you to the trailhead. In the winter, park in the day-use parking lot near Curry Village, and walk about 15 minutes to Happy Isles, where the trail begins. To reach the bridge looking out onto Vernal Fall, you'll walk 0.8 mile and gain 400 feet in elevation. To reach the falls' summits, there's a 1.5 mile hike with a 1,000-foot gain to Vernal Fall, and a 3.5 mile hike rising 1,900 feet to the top of Nevada Fall.

# What kinds of animals live in the park?

We have 370 different kinds of wildlife, but the total animal population is actually quite small. This is due in part to our making room for animals of another kind: four million visitors a year.

Our spring and summer skies are filled with the colors and songs of 247 species of birds. Among our well-known year-round residents are the acorn woodpecker, Steller's jay, and mountain chickadee.

Our rivers and lakes contain 12 species of fish, with just about every kind of trout, including cutthroat and rainbow. We also have a dozen types of frogs, toads, and salamanders, like the elusive Yosemite toad and limestone salamander. Hikers who are squeamish about snakes should make plenty of noise on the trail to scare away our 16 kinds of reptiles, including the king snake and western rattlesnake.

Visitors will see more birds than mammals, even though the furry folk outnumber our feathered friends almost ten to one. Of our 80 different types of mammals, you're most likely to see squirrels and chipmunks picking up scraps around visitor areas. You might glimpse a deer, coyote, or a black bear, but you will probably only catch the tracks of a badger, bobcat, fox, or mountain lion.

The National Park Service protects the natural habitats of the endangered and threatened species that are of special concern in California, including the Yosemite toad, Northern spotted owl, and Southern Willow flycatcher. The rangers have also started a series of programs to restore natural wildlife habitats and protect visitors from injury and property damage.

# What are the best ways to spot wildlife?

The chance to see Yosemite's wildlife increases with your ability to be patient and quiet. Losing the crowd doesn't hurt, either. Often, if you walk on a trail just one-half mile away from the sounds of busy visitor areas in the park, you begin to see signs of our animals. A group of people romping and singing across a meadow will scare our animals away, but the person who stays behind—watching and listening—can witness this same meadow come to life.

Darker fabrics blend more naturally with the surroundings. If you're walking, move slowly; if you see an animal, avoid sudden movements. Don't forget binoculars to give you that eagle-eye vision.

The best time to see wildlife is during the cool mornings and evenings of spring and summer, and the warmer midday hours of fall and winter. Animals are like people in that way, seeking out the most comfortable times of day to explore.

In the spring and summer, Yosemite is literally for the birds. Birders are well advised to leave their cars behind, get away from the roads, and become bird listeners as a thousand songs fill the air. In the winter, bald eagles descend upon Yosemite and are sometimes spotted around the unfrozen, middle-elevation lakes of Hetch Hetchy Reservoir and Lake Eleanor. Three pairs of peregrine falcons live in the park, giving springtime visitors a chance to see these rare birds in flight.

From the valley floor to elevations up to 9,000 feet, early

morning hikers might spot one of the park's snakes or lizards sunning itself on the trail. The western aquatic garter snake is the exception, often swimming in streams and ponds.

If you want to glimpse some of Yosemite's 16 kinds of fish, approach the task with the care and timing of a master angler. Waiting on a lake's shore or stream's edge, you can watch them feeding, making circles in the still waters of early morning or late afternoon.

Chipmunks and squirrels are easy to find at most elevations. Just hang around a campground or picnic area, and you'll see them gathering crumbs and other bits of trash—maybe even the food you still wanted. In the cool of the morning and early evening, mule deer are often seen grazing in small groups in the sunlit meadows and shadows of the oak groves. You might see coyote too, which hunt from the late afternoon on into the night.

Our black bears are surprisingly shy but are sometimes seen foraging in the mountainous areas of the park in the early morning or late evening. Some bears have discovered the food that people leave behind, so they sometimes rummage around campgrounds late at night.

Don't try to get too close to the animals in the park. Feeding a chipmunk might seem like a fun idea, but all it takes is one sick animal to infect others, including humans. Deer shouldn't eat people-food either. A diet of old bread and cookies can harm their digestive systems and the milk they pass to their fawns. As for the bears, don't ever get between a cub and its protective mama.

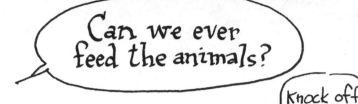

**Can we ever feed the animals?**

Knock off the fatty foods.

Every time someone feeds an animal in the park, a little bit of the "wild" is stolen from our wildlife. Human food can not only damage the animals' health but also can change their behavior and endanger their survival by luring them away from their natural habits (and into the roads!).

Federal law prohibits people from feeding or approaching the park's wildlife, and for good reason. Our animals may look harmless, but any one of them is capable of causing infection, injury—and in extreme cases even death—to people who get too close. If an animal is aware of your presence, you're probably too close.

Remember, keeping food to yourself helps keep our wildlife wild and healthy.

## Yosemite's Endangered or Threatened Species

**ENDANGERED (FEDERAL)**
California bighorn sheep
**THREATENED (FEDERAL)**
Spotted owl
**ENDANGERED
(STATE OF CALIFORNIA)**
Southern willow flycatcher
Peregrine falcon
Great grey owl
California bighorn sheep
**THREATENED
(STATE OF CALIFORNIA)**
Bald eagle
California wolverine
Sierra Nevada red fox
**SPECIES OF SPECIAL CONCERN
(STATE OF CALIFORNIA)**
Merlin

Osprey
Long-eared owl
Northern goshawk
Pallid bat
Sierra Nevada mountain beaver
Golden eagle
Yosemite toad
Townsend's big-eared bat
Western pond turtle
Spotted bat
Western mastiff bat
Mount Lyell salamander
**RARE PLANT SPECIES
(STATE OF CALIFORNIA)**
Congdon's lewisia
Congdon's woolly sunflower
Tompkin's sedge
Yosemite onion

# Is it true bears are the most dangerous animals?

**E**ven though bears are the most powerful wild animals in Yosemite, they are not the most dangerous to humans.

Does it surprise you to learn that the only death of a human by an animal in Yosemite's history was caused by a deer? Timid as they may seem, deer are wild animals, with sharp hooves and antlers that can strike swiftly and without warning. Bucks are especially dangerous during spring's mating season.

Most injuries to people result from trying to get too close to animals— like when they try to feed the squirrels and raccoons by hand and end up getting scratched and bitten. Fleas carried by ground squirrels have been known to spread disease, even the bubonic plague. So don't be fooled into thinking the little cute ones are harmless.

With no wolves remaining, the coyote is the largest native canid in California. Yosemite's coyotes are normally very shy, but they've become accustomed to all the visitors. Despite any resemblance they might have to your dog friends back home, they are wild and should be avoided.

With a natural fear of humans, mountain lions pose little threat to people in the park. These animals feed mostly on deer, a natural activity that helps keep our ecology in a delicate balance.

Because of their size and habits, Yosemite's black bears have a somewhat fearsome reputation. To be honest, some of it is deserved. Each year they cause more property damage than any other animal in the park. Let's just say it's best if people and bears maintain a "long-distance" relationship.

Year-round, Yosemite Valley is where you'll find most of our bird species. They're all around you, in the dry woodlands, humid forests, thickets, shrubby hillsides, boggy meadows, and grass-covered slopes. Watch for our rare birds, like eagles and falcons, that normally winter in the valley.

On the way to the Arch Rock Entrance, a winter drive along Highway 140 in the Merced River canyon will take you by a great birding spot around El Portal. Wandering around the chaparral, oak woodlands, and slopes, you'll hear the songs of many of our common birds that favor the area's mild winters.

In the higher elevations, you should check out the bird life around Ackerson Meadow (4,600 feet). This is the area along Ackerson Creek between the South and Middle Forks of the Tuolumne River. Although most of it is outside park boundaries, it's home to more than 150 species of birds (spring–fall).

During the spring and summer months, higher elevations like Tuolumne Meadows and along the Tioga Road are home to more than 140 bird species. If you're up for some high-altitude hiking, explore the bird habitats in the forests around Lembert and Pothole domes (9,000–9,400 feet) and the Hall Natural Area (10,000–13,000 feet).

If you forgot binoculars, you may be able to buy or rent a pair from Yosemite tour desks, lodgings, or retail shops.

**Enough about animals. What kinds of flora will we see?**

Yosemite is the land of evergreen. The various types of plants here outnumber our animal species three to one and come in as many shapes and sizes. Close your eyes in the meadow or forest; you'll hear the wind's voice in our more than 1,400 different plants and 37 types of trees. From the giant sequoia that rise nearly 300 feet in the air to ferns blanketing the forest floor, our world of flora is one of the park's greatest attractions.

Walk a few minutes from the Visitor Center and you'll pass through the sprawling shades of black and canyon oaks and see the tall ponderosa and a few lodgepole pines. Douglas firs and incense cedars flourish in the forests, with an occasional cottonwood, willow, alder, and azalea growing in moister areas.

Some of our pines have the sweet aroma of vanilla or pineapple, with long cones drooping like water drops from their upper branches. Our Pacific dogwood trees grow pale green flowers each spring, while the leaves of the quaking aspen turn golden in the fall.

The trails leading up out of the valley will bring you past sugar pines and white firs. Even higher, the flower-filled meadows and steep forest slopes are home to red firs and more sugar pines that reach 200 feet in the air.

Walking along Tuolumne Meadows, you'll leave oaks and firs behind. At this elevation the meadows rule, bordered by lodgepole pines and a scattering of mountain hemlocks, quaking aspens, and Sierra junipers.

Was it something I said?

# Where are the best places to see wildflowers?

Sprouting in the foothills in March, our wildflowers begin their six-month season. The valley blooms in May, and by August wildflowers spread their blanket of color to the park's high country.

As spring turns to summer, you can follow the blooms from Wawona Meadow in the south up to higher meadows like McGurk's and Mono. In the early spring, you'll find a great wildflower-covered trail starting at Savage's Trading Post in El Portal and leading up to the South Fork of the Merced. Around the same time, the violet family has moved into the valley. The Mountain Violet appears near Happy Isles and along the trail at Inspiration Point. The purple violet hangs out in the grass at the edge of Bridalveil Meadow, while the lone white violet keeps vigil in Leidig Meadow.

Summer brings azaleas to El Capitan Meadow and wild ginger along the trail from Mirror Lake to Snow Creek in Tenaya Canyon. Look for our pink to white pussy paws in the open, sunny flats of the valley, and the rose-and-silver tones of the showy milkweed in the valley's meadows.

By summer, the wildflowers have reached up into the rim country, where forests and meadows are crossed by streams and the two roads winding through wildflower havens. Take a walk along the rim country's trails or drive Glacier Point and Tioga Roads to get an eyeful of early summer color, like the bright red of the mountain pride, the glowing pink of the shooting star, or the brilliant yellow of the California coneflower. If you're up to the adventure, try the Pohono Trail for a 13-mile, all-day hike through some our mid-elevation's most awesome wildflower scenery.

In August, the high country gets its own share of color. Driving east on the Tioga Road to the park's Tioga Pass Entrance, you'll find a wildflower bounty around Tuolumne Meadows, beaming with the magenta of the Lemmon's paintbrush, the soft yellow of buttercups, and the indigo hue of whorled penstemon.

When you've hiked as high as you can go, you won't see any more trees, but you'll still find wildflowers. Some of the high country trails, like in Dana Meadows, just east of Tioga Pass, and Long Meadow, near the Sunrise High Sierra Camp, take you past some awesome blooms.

# When is the prime time to see fall color?

In the fall, of course! In October and November, the rich colors of our trees and meadows are enough to make your eyes water, the leaves so heavy with red, gold, and green that they simply have to fall.

There are certain places in the park where you're sure to catch the season's best sights. In El Capitan Meadow, sprawling black oaks drop their red and golden leaves into the Merced River; on its banks the alder trees stand tall with yellow-green leaves set against their white bark. Other spots provide a sampling of just about every fall color, like Cook's Meadow, where the black oak, maple, and white alder paint the sky. Sometimes one tree, like the dogwood, often dresses in fall's coat of many colors.

Autumn is a great time to walk in the valley. Try the Mirror Lake trail with its honey-colored carpet of leaves that follows along Tenaya Creek. At midday, the sun shines through the trees' branches to the forest floor.

The trails of the south and north rim country will take you past pocket meadows and scatterings of trees drenched in autumn color. If you drive the Tioga, Glacier Point, or Wawona roads, you'll see vast meadows turned to fields of gold.

## Where can we see a giant sequoia?

In the park there are three groves of giant sequoias, sometimes called Big Trees or Sierra redwoods. The largest of the three is the **Mariposa Grove** near Wawona at the southern border of the park. Here you can walk through the California Tunnel Tree—originally cut as a tourist attraction to allow horses and carriages to ride through. In the summer, you can take a narrated, one-hour Big Trees Tram Tour to see the major sites among the of hundreds of trees, including the nearly 3,000 year-old Grizzly Giant, with a branch that measures six feet around. Tickets can be bought at the Mariposa Gift Shop. You can drive to the trees on Mariposa Grove Road (summer–fall) but think about parking at the Wawona Store and riding the free shuttle bus to the Grove. In the winter and early spring, you will have to park at the South Entrance and walk the four miles round-trip to the grove since the road is closed.

**Tuolumne Grove** is another good place for giant-hunting. Here stands the Dead Giant, which one can walk through. You can reach Tuolumne Grove by foot from Crane Flat. Park in the Tuolumne Grove parking area on the Tioga Road (Hwy. 120 East) which is one mile east of Crane Flat. Just walk one mile in to view the grove!

Four miles west of the Tuolumne Grove is the **Merced Grove,** a little valley where wildflowers grow in spring and sequoias reach for the sky. Park at the Merced Grove trailhead off of the Big Oak Flat Road (Hwy. 120 West) and walk the four miles round-trip into the grove.

Many visitors confuse the giant sequoias with their cousins, the coast redwoods, which have bragging rights for having the tallest tree in the world. Besides the difference in appearance (the sequoias' reddish-gray bark compared to the deeper red color of the redwoods'), they grow in different regions. Redwoods are found between Northern California and Oregon on the coast, while sequoias grow inland on the western slopes of the Sierra Nevada.

The redwoods may have the tallest single tree, but our sequoias' trunks have the largest measured diameters of any tree trunk in the world.

Redwood. | Sequoia!

# What happened to the famous drive-through tree?

The story begins in 1878 with the tunneling of the first tree in Yosemite, a 29.5-foot tall sequoia tree stump called the "Dead Giant" in the Tuolumne Grove. Then, in 1881 a man named Albert Henry Washburn came along. As head of the Yosemite Stage and Turnpike Company and owner of the newly built Wawona Hotel, Washburn had a keen interest in tourist traffic. He set out to build a new road so visitors could travel with ease from the lower to the upper sequoia groves. There was one thing standing in his way: a 2,000 year-old, 234-foot tall giant sequoia.

Washburn, known as "the transportation king of the Sierra," would not be stopped. His team cut an 8-foot-wide, 10-foot-high, and 26-foot-long hole through the tree—big enough for a horse and wagon to roll through.

The Wawona Tunnel Tree quickly became a major park attraction, drawing visitors from around the world. But it was not to last. With a hole in the heart of its trunk and the adverse effects of a severe snowstorm, the sequoia fell in the winter of 1968–1969. It has now been renamed The Fallen Tunnel Tree.

Park visitors then turned more attention to the Dead Giant in the Tuolumne Grove, flocking to this tunnel tree until the summer of 1993, when park officials closed off car traffic due to damage to the grove's ecosystem. Today, only those on foot can go through the Dead Giant, and they can get there by taking the old Big Oak Flat Road from Crane Flat to Tuolumne Grove. In the Mariposa Grove, you can walk through the California Tunnel Tree, which is near the Grizzly Giant.

EXCUSE ME!! WHERE CAN WE DRIVE INTO A TREE?

PARK RANGER

# Are any of the plants poisonous?

**Y**ou should know that with all the different plants in Yosemite, it's only natural that some have a bit of a nasty side to them. Not to worry, though: any threat from these plants-with-attitudes is generally not serious and can easily be avoided with a little caution.

Poison oak dwells in the shady areas of the park's lower elevations. It's quite the chameleon, changing from green in spring to red in autumn, but it's almost always identifiable by its three leaves. The oil from this sneaky plant can cause a rash a few days after contact, at which time your skin will swell and itch. If you think you might have touched poison oak, wash your body with cold water and soap to close your pores and get rid of the oils. Tecnu, a poison-oak-specific soap, is a wise product to bring along with you on ANY camping trip!

Walking through the meadows in the valley, you might also feel the prickly sting of nettles. They hide in the meadow grasses, so keep a sharp eye out for where you're stepping in the fields. Rangers ask that you stick to established trails, to protect both the plants and yourselves!

Coming across wild mushrooms isn't dangerous, as long as you look instead of touch. Whatever you do, never eat a mushroom from the wild. If you touch one, like the deadly Amanitus, make sure you wash your hands thoroughly.

Pants and long sleeves will help if you decide to venture off-trail, or you can just stay clear of plant trouble altogether by sticking to the well-worn paths.

It's a jungle out there.

# What was life like for Yosemite's native peoples?

Imagine Yosemite long before it was a national park: no cars or roads, no buildings or parking lots, but water still plunging in great falls and wildflowers still blanketing the valley's meadows in spring. People were living here 4,000 years before the Spanish arrived and gold was discovered in the hills, and they called their home Ahwahnee ("place of a gaping mouth") and themselves, the Ahwahneechee. Today, we know them as the Yosemite Miwoks.

Until gold miners arrived in the mid 1800s, the Miwok people lived a relatively unchanged lifestyle in Yosemite. They gathered seeds and plants, hunted game, and traded with other tribes from the east. The Miwoks practiced very little cultivation, moving from the higher elevations in spring and summer to the warmer foothills and valley in fall and winter. This lifestyle proved to be very gentle on the land. Today, the traces of their existence are found in artifacts like obsidian tools and granite grinding rocks.

They built cedar bark homes and earth-covered gathering halls. Acorns provided a food staple, prepared and eaten as mush and combined with veggies like mushrooms, ferns, clover, and bulbs. With bows and arrows they hunted deer, rabbits, and squirrels and fished the rivers and streams for trout and Sacramento suckers. Some insects like fly larvae, caterpillars, and grasshoppers were delicacies.

To better understand Miwok life and the dramatic changes that took place when European Americans moved into the area, visit the re-created Indian Village and cultural exhibit near the Valley Visitor Center.

BEAR RIGHT.

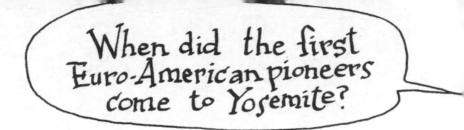

# When did the first Euro-American pioneers come to Yosemite?

**I**n 1851, a group of men formed a small army called the Mariposa Battalion to attack the Ahwahneechee, part of the southern Miwok, who had defended their homeland against gold miners settling in the area. The battalion drove the natives from Yosemite, and forever changed the land once known as Ahwahnee.

A San Franciscan (originally from England) named James Mason Hutchings read about the Mariposa Battalion in the newspaper and decided to see the place for himself. Inspired by the sight of Yosemite, Hutchings organized the first tourist party to the valley in 1855. The word was out.

Tourists, homesteaders, and folks with money on their mind flocked to the area—first on foot and horseback, then by wagon and stagecoach—and soon there were hotels, roads, homes, livestock, orchards, crops, and stores in the valley. By the late 1860s, the valley was bustling with private businesses cashing in on Yosemite's new-found popularity.

Overuse of the land worried some people. Early conservationists like I. W. Raymond and Frederick Law Olmstead, both with friends in high places, asked the government for help. By 1864, they got a bill passed by Congress and signed by President Abraham Lincoln giving Yosemite Valley and the Mariposa Grove of Big Trees to the state of California to preserve and protect. Yosemite became the world's first government-protected natural area, marking the beginning of the state and national park systems in the United States.

To learn more about the pioneer days in Yosemite, visit the Pioneer Yosemite History Center in Wawona. During the summer interpreters in period costumes introduce you to some of the people and events that shaped Yosemite's history. You can see historic buildings, a covered bridge and horse-drawn carriages. Check out your copy of the *Yosemite Guide* for demonstration times.

I preferred things the way they were before the last ice age.

PIONEER YOSEMITE HISTORY CENTER

As far as army posts go, they don't get much better than this. Soon after Congress declared Yosemite a national park on October 1, 1890, Captain A. E. Woods and his U.S. Army troops arrived in Yosemite to act as the original park caretakers and administrators. In 1914, the troops handed the reins over to the first civilian National Park Service staff, but not before paving the way for today's Yosemite.

In the spring of 1891, the army set up Camp A. E. Woods just north of Wawona, along with many small patrol camps around the park. Their first battle was against the sheepherders, whose livestock was chowing down on Yosemite's high country. Next came the dirty work of preparing a national park.

They covered every inch of the park, mapping and marking its boundaries, blazing trails and building bridges, stocking lakes and rivers, fighting fires, and confiscating guns from unruly visitors and residents.

By 1906, it was time to further civilize the valley. Captain Harry C. Benson and his 6th Cavalry established Fort Yosemite on the site where the Yosemite Lodge sits today and quickly got down to the business of building sanitation facilities to stop raw sewage from polluting streams and rivers. They also rid the valley of firearms and animal traps laid by settlers, and in 1912 they built the Yosemite Hospital. The next year, the first automobiles started rolling into the valley, so the troops enforced the speed limits of 15 miles per hour in the valley and five miles per hour on steep descents.

The Army left behind their bridges, their trails, their maps...

...An their hate

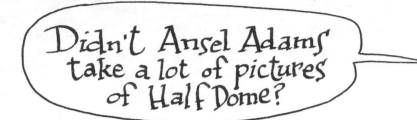

**Didn't Ansel Adams take a lot of pictures of Half Dome?**

Ansel Adams did take many famous photographs of Yosemite, including ones of Half Dome. He first set foot in the park in 1916, armed with a new gift: a box camera. By the late 1920s, Adams was working for the Yosemite Park and Curry Company, which hired him to take pictures of the park for newspapers and magazines. It was the beginning of a life-long love for Yosemite and also the start of his efforts as a leading conservationist in California.

Adams's photographs became famous worldwide. Even after his death in 1984, his pictures live on, and many visitors still flock to the park just to see the images that he captured through his lens.

Today, Adams's original artwork can be admired and purchased at the Ansel Adams Gallery (209/372-4413, www.anseladams.com), next to the Visitor Center in Yosemite Village. The gallery also features work by other photographers and fine artists, rents cameras and leads camera walks so you can search for your own Yosemite masterpiece.

## What can I take home as a memento of my visit?

**W**ith an awe-inspiring backdrop like Yosemite, anyone with a camera can take home some of the magic without stealing anything away from the beauty of the park. There are no mementos quite like the photographs which capture and give life to special memories, such as that of a snowshoed walk through Tuolumne Meadows or a hike up Mist Trail.

For less adventuresome keepsakes, check out the park shops, galleries, and museums. Besides the ever-popular T-shirts and mugs, there are a wide range of gifts that evoke the spirit of Yosemite, including jewelry carved with the images of local flora and fauna, candles with pressed wildflowers, Native American arrowheads and crafts, and everything Ansel Adams, from post-cards to original prints selling for thousands of dollars.

The search for souvenirs can become a problem in our park. That's why people are prohibited from destroying or removing just about everything in the park, including plants, animals, minerals, and archeological artifacts. A family driving out with a basketful of pine cones shouldn't be surprised if the ranger hands over a $50–100 citation—one of the less desirable of Yosemite mementos.

These regulations are designed to keep Yosemite intact despite the four million visitors a year who want to take a piece of it home. Just think, if everyone started chipping away a piece of Half Dome, it would soon become Quarter Dome.

NOW WHAT?

## What's the best way to see the park?

### Free Shuttles

I'll bet John Muir never would have guessed there'd one day be a shuttle in Yosemite Valley taking people wherever they wanted to go. We haven't figured out how to get one up Half Dome yet, but we do have a shuttle that goes to 19 other popular spots in Yosemite Valley. This is the only year-round free shuttle, and it operates 7 A.M.–10 P.M. arriving at each stop every 15–30 minutes during the busy summer and every 30 minutes in the winter. Remember, you're one of 25,000 riders in the peak season, so be ready to wait in line.

In summer you can catch a shuttle to El Capitan on the hour and half-hour from 9 A.M.–6 P.M. at Valley Visitor Center (shares Valley shuttle stop #5), El Capitan Picnic Area, El Capitan Meadow and the Four-Mile Trail trailhead.

In Wawona, a free shuttle picks up passengers at the South Entrance station, Mariposa Grove Gift Shop and Wawona Store (spring–fall). Keep in mind that when the parking lots fill up in the summer the Mariposa Grove Road closes several times a day! If you are on one of the free shuttle buses you can still get in to see the Grove even when the parking lots are closed.

In summer free shuttles are available in Tuolumne Meadows every half-hour (7 A.M.–7 P.M.), taking visitors from the Tuolumne Meadows Lodge to the Olmsted Point, with 10 stops in between. The shuttle also provides service between the Tuolumne Meadows Lodge and Tioga Pass (limited hours).

Skiers can ride a shuttle to and from the Badger Pass slopes from Yosemite Valley, with three other stops, whenever the Badger Pass facilities are open.

### Tram Tours

A two-hour ranger-narrated park tour in an open-air tram (weather permitting) costs $22 for adults, $18 for seniors, and $11.50 for children over five, and operates spring–fall. In the winter you will enjoy an enclosed and heated motor coach. The tour starts at Yosemite Lodge at the Falls (shuttle stop #8).

In the summer, Wawona has a daily, one-hour-and-fifteen minute tram tour through the Mariposa Grove called the Big Trees Tram Tour. It boards at Mariposa Grove and cost is $16 for adults, $14 for seniors, and $11 for children over five.

### Bus Tours

Year-round you can take a Yosemite Valley Floor tour (two hours, $22 for adults, $11.50 for children). Late spring–early fall, buses run from Yosemite

Lodge to Glacier Point ($32.50 for adults, $26 for seniors, $26 for children), to and from Tuolumne Meadows (eight hours, $23 for adults, $11.50 for children), and around the valley by moonlight during the full moon (two hours, $22 for adults, $18 for seniors and $11.50 for children). If you are ready for an all-day tour to see all the hot spots you can take the Yosemite Grand Tour, with or without lunch ($62 for adults, $55 for seniors, and $33 for children, prices do not include the lunch option). Current times and dates will be listed in your *Yosemite Today* and at any Tour and Activity Desk.

To make reservations before you get to the park and to learn more about fees call 209/372-4386 or go online to www.yosemitepark.com/Activities_GuidedBusTours.aspx to get more information.

## Autos

Determined drivers can visit quite a few park areas, many with turnouts and informational signs. You can buy a 2–4-hour audio tour of the park at the Valley Visitor Center. Remember, Yosemite Valley and the Mariposa Grove always have tons of traffic, and cars are not allowed on the Happy Isles Loop, Mirror Lake/Meadow roads, or the roads through Yosemite Village. For road conditions, call 209/372-0200.

## Bikes

With over 12 miles of well-marked bike paths, bicycling is a fun and safe way to get around the park; just stay on the paved paths and roads, and wear a helmet. You can rent bikes and helmets by the hour or for the day at the Yosemite Lodge or Curry Village, conditions permitting.

## Walking

The best way to escape the crowds and see Yosemite's finer points is to hoof it, hiking or backpacking through some of the 800 miles of developed trails within park boundaries. These hikes range from easy walks along the valley floor to steeper treks to Upper Yosemite Falls, Mirror Lake, and Vernal Fall. You should know your limits before embarking on one of these journeys, and remember to bring water. You might want to stop at the Wilderness Center next to the post office in Yosemite Village to learn about some paths.

## Other Options

Cross-country skiing and snowshoeing are great ways to traverse the park during the snowy months. In the summer, you can let a horse do all the work on two-hour, four-hour, or all-day rides that start from the stables in Wawona and Tuolumne Meadows. There are no longer any stables in Yosemite Valley. Children must be age seven or older to ride.

## Where are the Yosemite Valley shuttle bus stops?

Almost anywhere you find yourself in the eastern end of the valley there's a shuttle bus stop nearby. Buses run every 15–30 minutes or so (7 A.M.–10 P.M., spring–fall). In the winter, the buses run every 30 minutes, and they do not visit shuttle stops #15, #16, #17 or #18.

There are stops that access the major campgrounds, Yosemite Lodge, Camp Curry and the Ahwahnee Hotel, Yosemite Village with all its services and shops, and some of the more scenic trails in the valley. The buses even take you to areas such as Happy Isles and Mirror Lake, which are closed to private automobiles.

## Here's a list of the shuttle stops:

| | |
|---|---|
| 1 | Yosemite Village/Day Parking |
| 2 | Yosemite Village |
| 3 | The Ahwahnee Hotel |
| 4 | Yosemite Village/Degnan's Complex |
| 5 | Valley Visitor Center/El Capitan Shuttle Link |
| 6 | Lower Yosemite Fall |
| 7 | Camp 4/Upper Yosemite Fall Trailhead |
| 8 | Yosemite Lodge |
| 9 | Valley Visitor Center |
| 10 | Yosemite Village |
| 11 | Sentinel Bridge/Parking for Yosemite Chapel |
| 12 | Housekeeping Camp/LeConte Memorial |
| 13A | Curry Village Rental Center |
| 13B | Curry Village Registration Desk |
| 14 | Curry Village Parking |
| 15 | Upper Pines Campground |
| 16 | Happy Isles/John Muir Trailhead |
| 17 | Mirror Lake Junction |
| 18 | Stables |
| 19 | Lower Pines Campground |
| 20 | Curry Village Parking |
| 21 | Curry Village Rental Center |

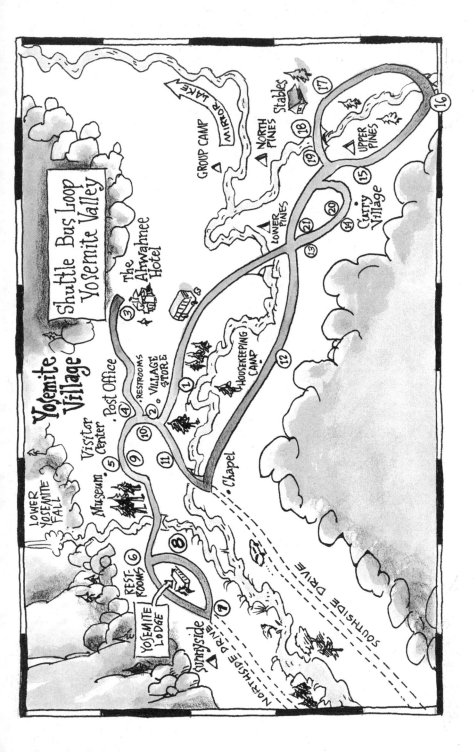

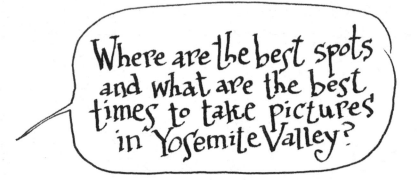

Where are the best spots and what are the best times to take pictures in Yosemite Valley?

Whether an autumn leaf or the heights of Half Dome, a great subject for a memorable Yosemite snapshot is around every turn. The light will bring these pictures to life, and every hour of the day offers different shading.

Yosemite and Nevada Falls go through many changes in the course of a day. At mid-morning, the sun casts shadows and light on the falling water. Later in the afternoon, the falls cast their own shadows on the cliff and stand out clearly from the rock face.

Spring is the best season to capture our waterfalls. At Bridalveil Fall, the shadows lift at midday to reveal a sunlit mist at its top that helps people understand its name.

A stroll from the Happy Isles Nature Center to Vernal Fall reaps photo riches between the hours of 10 A.M.–noon, with the light changing the water into falling jewels.

During spring, Mirror Lake lives up to its name until about 8 A.M., when the sun steals its reflection. Don't be discouraged if the day is overcast; on a cloudy day the lake's mirror is often at its clearest, and the light has a nice even tone by which to take shots of the lake's scenic views of Half Dome.

The fun part is finding your own perfect scene to capture on film. From El Capitan to a secret trail, your memories of the park's beauty are only a click away. Contact the Ansel Adams Gallery (209/372-4413) to sign up for a free photography walk at least two days before you plan to arrive, the spaces are limited to just 25 people. All levels of skill are welcome and the walk lasts from 1.5–2 hours.

One of the best places in the Valley to take pictures is behind the camera!

## Are there any self-guided tours?

Y ou'll find plenty of ways to lead your own tours in the
park. You can start in the Yosemite Museum, where you'll learn about
Yosemite's human and natural history, then take the one-mile Changing
Yosemite nature walk trail.

History buffs can visit the museum's American Indian cultural exhibit, then take a short, self-guided walk through a re-created Miwok Indian
village. The Pioneer Yosemite History Center in Wawona offers a 30-minute, self-guided tour that reveals the lifestyles of Yosemite's early pioneers.

Self-guided tours also let you venture into the wild. Yosemite has a
number of walking trails with signs along the way, teaching visitors about
plant life, native animals, history, and special geographic features. Giant
sequoia seekers can take a half-mile, self-guided tour of Tuolumne Grove
or the slightly longer walk through Mariposa Grove, which leads to the
famous Grizzly Giant. The Pioneer Yosemite History Center in Wawona
has a self-guided tour around the historical structures and markers. You
can download brochures on both trails at www.nps.gov/yose/planyour-
visit/brochures.htm before you arrive at the park.

Do-it-yourself road adventures are found in the pages of the
*Yosemite Road Guide* ($3.50), which steers you to more than 120
roadside markers, each offering interesting bits of information about
Yosemite's natural features and history.

The newest addition to the list of self-guided tours is a handheld
GPS tour that takes you on a two-hour walk on the Lower Falls Tour.
By using the Explorer device you can learn 50 stories about the locations and history along the path and play an interactive game if you
wish—videos and clips are GPS sensor activated or manually activated.
Be sure to ask about a group discount if you have 10 or more people in
your party. Cost is $9.95 for adults and $7.95 for kids—headphone rental is an additional $1 or you can use your own.
The devices can be rented at the Yosemite Valley Visitor
Center bookstore.

Um...
tree!

The best way to unlock the mysteries of Yosemite is to hang out with the people that have the keys: the Yosemite rangers, the ones wearing Smokey-the-Bear hats. Your best resource is to check the Scheduled Events section in your copy of *Yosemite Today*—departure times, durations, subject and locations of the ranger-led walks are all clearly listed.

In the valley, rangers lead a series of free 1.5–2-hour narrated walks, or Ranger Strolls, on various subjects, including wildlife, geography, and park history. Most of these informative tours start from the Yosemite Museum or the Valley Visitor Center. Guides are also on hand to lead visitors on a few unique walks, like the one that focuses on the history of climbing in Yosemite and another that features the best places to take pictures. There is even a stroll led by a guide who looks and acts just like John Muir.

Mariposa Grove rangers lead visitors on 1.5-hour walks through the grove in the summer, explaining the many wonders of the sequoia forests. Walks start from the trailhead parking lot several times each day. The Wawona Information Station offers similar

tours of the area, led by naturalists and park historians. Check the bulletin board at the Mariposa Grove trailhead, or call the Wawona Information Station at 209/375-9501.

The magical red fir forests and awesome views at Glacier Point become even more amazing on 2–3.5-hour ranger walks. Everyday in the winter, there is a two-hour ranger-led snowshoe walk at the Badger Pass ski area that helps visitors discover how the park's plants and animals survive the harsh Sierra winters. Snowshoes are provided for a small donation.

In Tuolumne Meadows, rangers lead morning, noon, and afternoon nature walks ranging from 1–8 hours in length. There are two-hour Junior Ranger programs as well for kids ages 7–12. You can picnic with your guide while you learn about the natural and human history of Yosemite's subalpine areas. For information on all of these walks, call the Tuolumne Meadows Visitor Center at 209/372-0263 (summer only).

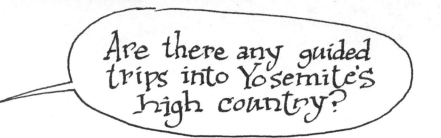

Are there any guided trips into Yosemite's high country?

A journey into Yosemite's high country isn't exactly a walk in the valley. You need to be in good shape to tackle these trails and should plan on spending a day prior to your trip acclimating to the higher elevations.

For those ready to take on a three-day or four-day guided trip outside of the valley starting at $300—including meals, tents, stove and water filters—contact the Yosemite Mountaineering School (yms@dncinc.com), or visit their website (www.yosemitepark.com/Activities_HikingCamping_OvernightBackpackingTrips.aspx).

For those ready to take on a week-long hike, there's a guided tour covering 5–10 miles each day, stopping at five High Sierra Camps and climbing over ten thousand feet. Experienced rangers lead these high country excursions which embark four times a week from the Tuolomne Meadows lodge (June–early Sept.). The cost is approximately $1100 per person for six nights lodging and all meals. For more information, call the High Sierra desk at (209)253-5674.

You can also experience high country excitement sitting atop a saddle. Scenic horseback trips, led by knowledgeable guides, depart daily on two-hour, half-day, and all-day rides from Yosemite Valley, Wawona and Tuolumne Meadows (June–Labor Day). If you don't get too saddle-sore, you can try a four-day or six-day saddle tour into the high country. Prices include lodging and all meals at the High Sierra Camps. For more information and reservations, call 559/253-5674.

In winter, you can glide your way across the high country slopes by taking a cross-country ski tour with the Badger Pass ski school. For more details, call 209/372-8444.

Whew!

# How does winter change getting around in the park?

Winter's big freeze closes off Tioga Road and Glacier Point Road (from Badger Pass ski area). With the help of a snowplow, the rest of the park stays open all winter, unless there's a monster snowfall that makes it impossible to clear the roads.

Highway 140, going through Merced, Mariposa, and the Arch Rock Entrance, seems to get the least of winter's fury. Highways 120 and 41 from the west often get a heavy dose of snow, requiring drivers to practice their skills at putting on tire chains. But once you're in the valley, you can usually rely on the snowplows doing their job.

We try to keep the Tioga and Glacier Point Roads open until November 1, but we've had some nasty snowstorms close these routes as early as September. Rockslides, fires, and other problems pop up every now and then to cause closures, as well.

Winter driving in Yosemite can be dangerous. With the roads covered with snow and hard-to-see ice, you'll need to slow down and carry a set of chains at all times. Keep a sharp eye out for snowplows, and use those turnouts if you need to stop for a while. For 24-hour road conditions in Yosemite, call 209/372-0200.

# Is there a shuttle out of the Valley?

If you want to start high and hike downhill there are two buses you can take to get you out of the valley. A two-hour bus ride will take you from the Yosemite Lodge at the Falls (shuttle stop #8) from the valley up 3,200 feet to Glacier Point. This is a tour bus on which hikers can get a one-way ticket then select a trail back to the valley. Trail maps are sold at the Glacier Point store.

The Glacier Point Tour leaves daily in the summer from the Yosemite Lodge at 8:30 A.M., 10 A.M., and 1:30 P.M. (one-way trip, $20 for adults, $18 for seniors, $12 for children ages five and older, free for children under five).

Before you get to the park you can make reservations up to seven days in advance by calling DNC at 559/252-4848. Once you are in the park you make reservations at any Tour and Activity Desk. Reservations are not required but they are highly recommended in the summer months—you can try to show up early at the Yosemite Lodge at the Falls to see if tickets are available.

If Tuolomne Meadows is your destination you can catch the Tuolumne Meadows bus at Curry Village (shuttle stop #13B) at 8 A.M., next to the Fire House in Yosemite Village at 8:05 A.M. (shuttle stop #2), and at the Yosemite Lodge at 8:20 A.M. (shuttle stop #8). This summer-only bus runs round-trip ($23 for adults and $11.50 for children) but you can ride it one-way ($14.50 for adults and $7.25 for children). The same reservations guidelines apply as for the Glacier Point Tour.

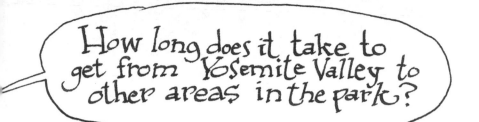

# How long does it take to get from Yosemite Valley to other areas in the park?

For most visitors, the valley is the perfect springboard for other park excursions. To get to other areas, follow the "All Park Exits" signs leading to a one-way road out of the valley. From here, you'll see exit signs for Highway 41 to Fresno, 140 to Merced, 120 to Manteca, and 120 east to the Tioga Road.

Heading south on Highway 41 (Wawona Road), you travel about an hour to get to Glacier Point (closed in winter) or Wawona and the Pioneer Yosemite History Center. A short drive south from Wawona, you'll arrive at the Mariposa Grove of Big Trees, where you can park and take the shuttle or walk into the grove. (In the summer you should plan to park your car in Wawona and take the free shuttle to the Mariposa Grove.)

Taking Highway 120 (Big Oak Flat Road) westward, you'll reach Crane Flat in about 30 minutes. A bit further and you'll arrive at the Tuolumne and Merced Groves of Big Trees. It's a steep, two-mile, round-trip hike to Tuolumne Grove and a four-mile round-trip walk to Merced Grove. Near the Big Oak Flat Entrance, you can turn right toward Hetch Hetchy (no vehicles over 25 feet in length), an 1.5-hour drive from the valley.

Take Highway 120 (Tioga Road) to the east (closed in winter) for one hour to White Wolf, Tenaya Lake, and, after 1.5 hours, Tuolumne Meadows. Just 15 minutes more and you'll cross the highest paved pass in the Sierra: the nearly 10,000-foot Tioga Pass.

# IV
# Lodging
# and
# Dining

Where can we stay in the park?

After a long day roaming around Yosemite, a hot shower and a comfortable bed can do wonders for you. Luckily, you have close to 1,500 overnight accommodations in the park to choose from. Reservations for most lodgings are made through **DNC Parks & Resorts at Yosemite, Inc.** (559/253-5636, www.yosemitepark.com/Reservations.aspx).

## Yosemite Valley

If you're willing to pay for comfort, the **Ahwahnee Hotel** can be mighty tempting. This National Historic Landmark is the lap of luxury, with 123 rooms, views of Glacier Point and the valley's south wall, private cottages, and prices ranging from $426 for a standard room to $893 for a three-room suite. It's truly fit for a queen, as the Queen of England decided when she stayed in the penthouse in 1983. There are slightly reduced rates Sunday–Thursday in the winter months.

One of the 249 rooms in the **Yosemite Lodge** is a good choice after your excursions to nearby attractions like Yosemite Falls and the Merced River. Prices range from $177 for deluxe rooms with balconies to $147 for standard rooms with baths. The lodge with pool and many services is open year-round.

For more modest digs and prices, **Curry Village** has rooms with baths for around $147 during the high season, cabins with private ($120) and shared ($93) baths, and canvas tent cabins with communal baths that are heated ($78) and unheated ($74). It's open year-round, with reduced motel and cabin rates in the winter season, and is close to Glacier Point and Happy Isles.

**Housekeeping Camp** is a camping experience with a few basic amenities. For about $76 you get one of the 226 campsites that can accommodate up to six people. The sites feature a sleeping area with three concrete walls, concrete floor and a double canvas roof with a fourth curtained wall. The covered patio has a picnic table, bear-proof food storage container and a privacy fence. The shelter is furnished with a double bed, bunk beds, chairs, table, mirror, electric lights and outlets. Be sure to bring linens, sleeping bags, and cooking supplies. If you wish, bedpacks with two sheets, two blankets, and two pillows are available for rent at $2.50 a night. Located next to the Merced River, Housekeeping Camp also offers public showers, a store, shuttle stop, parking area and a laundromat. It is only open in summer.

## South Yosemite

The **Wawona Hotel** (559/253-5636) is another National Historic Landmark; it's also the oldest resort hotel in California. The Wawona offers old-fashioned luxury: Victorian buildings, 104 rooms and cottages, wide porches looking out on green lawns, a swimming pool, tennis courts, and a nine-hole golf course. The rooms with private baths cost $183, and those that share a community bathroom cost $126 during the high season. It's open early March–October, plus weekends and holidays through Christmas.

The **The Redwoods in Yosemite** (209/375-6666, www.redwoodsin yosemite.com) are privately owned vacation homes available by the day or week, all with kitchens and fireplaces. Costs range $132–469 per night, year-round. Eight miles from Badger Pass and a 30-minute drive from the valley, **Yosemite West Reservations** (559/642-2211) has homes and condominiums with TVs, kitchens, and range ovens. Price ranges $85–325 per night, year-round. Call for information and reservations.

## North Yosemite

The park's northern region offers accommodations in the summer only. On the road to Hetch Hetchy, the **Evergreen Lodge** (209/379-2606, www.evergreenlodge.com) has 21 rustic cabins (with baths) sleeping two people ($99–199) or up to four people ($119–259), with satellite radio, DVD players and DVD library included. There are no kitchens, but a restaurant, tavern, and small store are nearby.

**White Wolf Lodge** located 30 miles from Yosemite Valley also has four rustic cabins with private baths ($105 with $10 for each additional adult), 24 canvas tent cabins ($73, with $10 for each additional adult and $6 for each additional child) with shared bath and shower facilities, and a dining room and store—they are closed in the winter. Near the Tuolumne River, the **Tuolumne Meadows Lodge** has 69 canvas tent cabins ($78, with $10 for each additional adult and $6 for each additional child) with four beds, linens, a wood stove, wood and candles (no electricity). Bathrooms and showers are communal. This place is popular, so reserve early. You can book rooms at both of these lodges by calling 559/253-5635.

# The Ahwahnee Hotel

**CELEBRITIES WHO HAVE STAYED AT THE AHWAHNEE HOTEL:**
Ansel Adams, frequently between 1927 and his death in 1984
President Herbert Hoover in 1927, 1953, and 1960
President Franklin D. Roosevelt in 1938
Walt Disney in 1941
King Baudoin of Belgium in 1959
President John F. Kennedy in 1962
Queen Elizabeth II of England and Prince Philip in 1983
Actor Mel Gibson in 1992, during the filming of *Maverick*
Sir Edmund Hillary, 1995 and 1996
Actor Robert Redford, a frequent visitor to the hotel
Actors Brad Pitt and Jennifer Aniston in 2001

**FUNNY CELEBRITY STORIES:**

- Ahwahnee guests complained one evening about the loud music coming from the hotel lounge. The manager reluctantly asked Lucille Ball and Judy Garland to stop singing and playing the piano.

- When former president Herbert Hoover returned one afternoon from a day of fishing, a new Ahwahnee doorman politely turned him away due to Hoover's inappropriate attire.

**OTHER NATIONAL PARK PROJECTS DESIGNED BY THE AHWAHNEE HOTEL ARCHITECT, GILBERT STANLEY UNDERWOOD:**

- The Lodge at Zion National Park

- Canyon Lodge at Bryce Canyon National Park

- North Rim Lodge at Grand Canyon National Park

## Are there any convenient places to stay outside Yosemite?

No matter what direction you're coming from, there are lots of places to stay just outside the park's four entrances.

### Highway 41 from Fresno

*18 miles from the south entrance, in Oakhurst:*

| | |
|---|---|
| **Oakhurst Lodge**<br>888/431-9907, oklodge@sti.net | 60 units<br>$70 winter, $95–105 summer |
| **Shilo Inn**<br>559/683-3555, www.shiloinns.com | 80 units, pool<br>$69–154 winter,<br>$99–204 summer |
| **Yosemite Gateway Best Western**<br>559/683-2378,<br>www.yosemitegatewayinn.com | 122 units, 2 pools and spas<br>$54–112 winter,<br>$100–160 summer |

*4 miles from the south entrance, in Fish Camp:*

| | |
|---|---|
| **Marriott's Tenaya Lodge**<br>888/514-2167, www.tenayalodge.com | 122 units, 2 pools and a fitness center, skating rink in winter, dog friendly<br>$119–260 winter,<br>$225–379 summer |
| **Narrow Gauge Inn**<br>888/644-9050, www.narrowgaugeinn.com | 26 units, seasonal pool and hot tub, pet friendly<br>$79 and up winter,<br>$140–295 summer |
| **Apple Tree Inn**<br>559/683-5111,<br>www.appletreeinn-yosemite.com | 53 rooms with lovely gardens, indoor pool, spa, and racquetball court<br>$99–219 winter,<br>$159–259 summer (add $30 during holiday periods) |

YOSEMITE

## Highway 120 (east) from Lee Vining

*14 miles from the eastern entrance, in Lee Vining:*

| | |
|---|---|
| **Lakeview Lodge**<br>760/647-6543, 800/990-6614,<br>www.lakeviewlodgeyosemite.com | 46 units,<br>minimum three-night stay<br>$69–95 winter,<br>$99–142 summer |
| **Yosemite Gateway Motel**<br>760/647-6467,<br>www.yosemitegatewaymotel.com | 18 units<br>$59–79 winter,<br>$99–179 summer |

## Highway 140 from Merced

*32 miles from the Arch Rock Entrance, in Mariposa:*

| | |
|---|---|
| **Best Western Yosemite Way Station**<br>209/966-7545, www.yosemiteresorts.us | 77 rooms with pool,<br>spa, pets allowed<br>$65–69 winter, $80–105 summer |
| **Mariposa Lodge**<br>800/966-8819, www.mariposalodge.com | 45 units, pool, pets allowed<br>$69–89 winter,<br>$89–129 summer |
| **Mother Lode Lodge**<br>209/966-2521, www.mariposamotel.com | 14 units, pool<br>$49–99 winter, $59–109 summer |

*2–8 miles from the Arch Rock Entrance, in El Portal:*

| | |
|---|---|
| **Cedar Lodge**<br>888/742-4371, www.yosemiteresorts.us | 211 units, pools<br>$99–135 all year |
| **Yosemite View Lodge**<br>209/379-2681, 888/742-4371 | 335 units with three outdoor<br>pools and one indoor pool<br>$119–270 double,<br>$189–689 suite all year |

## Highway 120 from Manteca

*12 miles from the West Gate Entrance, in Buck Meadows:*

| | |
|---|---|
| **Buck Meadows Lodge**<br>209/962-5281 | 11 units<br>$69–89 all year |
| **Yosemite Westgate Lodge**<br>800/253-9673,<br>www.yosemitewestgate.com | 44 units, pool with spa<br>$49–165 all year |

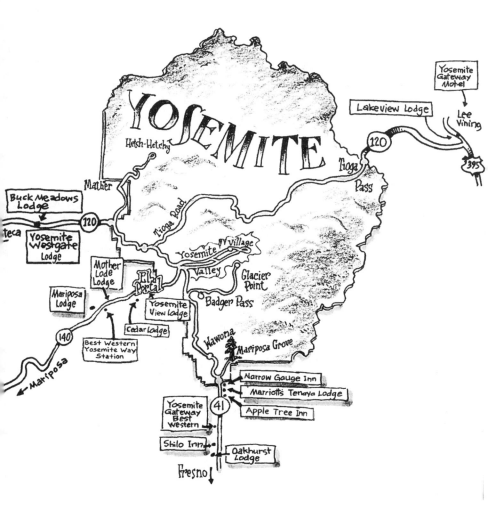

Where can we eat in the park?

## YOSEMITE VALLEY

### Yosemite Lodge at the Falls (shuttle stop #8)

The Lodge's **Food Court** offers inexpensive meals year-round for breakfast, lunch, and dinner—pasta, pizza, a grill and sandwiches. For a full-service restaurant with great views, try the **Mountain Room.** It has moderate-to-expensive prices, emphasis on local organic ingredients, steaks and seafood. Reservations are available for groups larger than eight people—call 209/372-1274. The **Mountain Room Lounge** offers light appetizers and cocktails—in the summer there is seating on the outdoor deck.

### Yosemite Village (shuttle stops #4 and #10)

Try **Degnan's Deli** for sandwiches, snacks, soups and salads; **Degnan's Café** offers coffee drinks and pastries; or go to **Degnan's Loft** for Italian fare including pizza, lasagne and salads. **Village Grill** (shuttle stop #2) serves inexpensive burgers, chicken sandwiches and the like with an outdoor seating area.

### Curry Village (shuttle stops #13A, #13B, #14 and #20)

The **Curry Village Pavilion** has a real mountain feel, with a chuckwagon barbeque line in the summer, a rustic atmosphere, and inexpensive prices. Inside the Pavilion, you can grab a cappuccino and pastries at the **Curry Village Coffee Corner,** which also offers ice cream after 11 A.M. **The Curry Bar** has burgers and fries, cocktails and signature strawberry margaritas all day, spring–fall, and the **Pizza Deck**—you guessed it—serves pizza on a deck, spring–fall, and has beer on tap, table service and great views. Feel like a taco, burrito or nachos in paradise? Stop by the **Taqueria,** located between the gift shop and the mountain shop inside Curry Village, for a quick bite.

PIZZA!
PIZZA!

## The Ahwahnee (shuttle stop #3)

Almost as great as Yosemite's natural treasures is a meal in the **Ahwahnee Dining Room** (209/372-1489). Breakfast and lunch are casual dress, but coats and ties are preferred at dinner. Prices are moderate to expensive. Dinner reservations are a must. **The Ahwahnee Bar** offers a limited menu, the same one you'll find poolside, and live music on most Fridays and Saturdays nights.

## SOUTH YOSEMITE

The **Wawona Hotel Dining Room** (559/253-5686) provides the area's only full-service fine dining. Lunch and Sunday brunch are served buffet style, and in the summer you can try the Saturday barbecue on the hotel lawn (moderate to expensive). Dinner reservations required. At the Wawona **Golf Shop Snack Bar,** you can watch the golfers while you munch on hot dogs, sandwiches, and other simple fare. Open summer and fall, the **Glacier Point Snack Stand** offers some basic menu items.

## NORTH YOSEMITE

On Evergreen Road toward Hetch Hetchy, the **Evergreen Lodge** (209/379-2606) serves simple and tasty dishes seven nights a week, plus breakfast on weekends April–October (moderate to expensive). Call for reservations. The **White Wolf Lodge** (559/252-4848) has fireside breakfasts and dinners (moderate to expensive) and an outdoor patio. Dinner reservations are recommended. Even though it's two miles outside the park, the **Tioga Pass Resort** (760/647-6423) is legendary to Yosemite visitors. There might be a bit of a wait for the moderately priced, all-day dining, but their homemade pie is worth it. Of the five High Sierra Camps in the park, **Tuolumne Meadows Lodge** (559/252-4848) is the only one accessible by car. The dining room is in a tentlike structure, but breakfasts and dinners are first class. Box lunches are available upon request. Call for required reservations. For reasonably priced high country chow, the **Tuolumne Meadows Grill** serves it up hot for breakfast, lunch, dinner, and orders to go. No reservations are accepted.

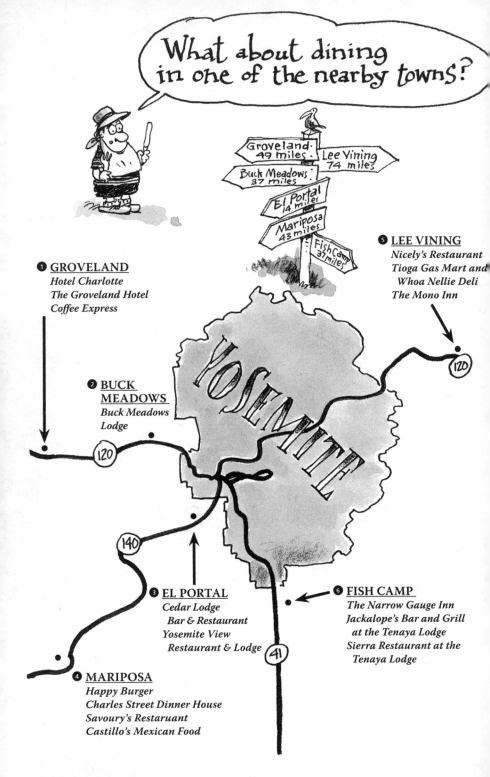

What about dining in one of the nearby towns?

Groveland 49 miles
Lee Vining 74 miles
Buck Meadows 37 miles
El Portal 14 miles
Mariposa 43 miles
Fish Camp 37 miles

**❶ GROVELAND**
*Hotel Charlotte*
*The Groveland Hotel*
*Coffee Express*

**❷ BUCK MEADOWS**
*Buck Meadows Lodge*

**❸ EL PORTAL**
*Cedar Lodge*
*Bar & Restaurant*
*Yosemite View*
*Restaurant & Lodge*

**❹ MARIPOSA**
*Happy Burger*
*Charles Street Dinner House*
*Savoury's Restaruant*
*Castillo's Mexican Food*

**❺ LEE VINING**
*Nicely's Restaurant*
*Tioga Gas Mart and*
*Whoa Nellie Deli*
*The Mono Inn*

**❻ FISH CAMP**
*The Narrow Gauge Inn*
*Jackalope's Bar and Grill*
*at the Tenaya Lodge*
*Sierra Restaurant at the*
*Tenaya Lodge*

# ❶ GROVELAND
(49 miles from the Yosemite Valley):

## Hotel Charlotte
Hearty California country food, steak, chicken, and daily specials
18736 Main St., 209/962-6455

## The Groveland Hotel
California cuisine with local beers and wine, special desserts
18933 Main St., 209/962-4000

## Coffee Express
Great homemade pies and sandwiches; breakfast and lunch only
Main St., 209/962-7393

# ❷ BUCK MEADOWS
(37 miles from the Yosemite Valley):

## Buck Meadows Lodge
Homestyle food, friendly service
7633 Hwy. 120, 209/962-5281

# ❸ EL PORTAL
(14 miles from the Yosemite Valley):

## Cedar Lodge Bar & Restaurant
'50s-era diner with burgers
9966 Hwy. 140, 209/379-2316

## Yosemite View Restaurant & Lounge
At the Yosemite View Lodge, family restaurant with pizza parlor
11136 Hwy. 140, 209/379-2681

# ❹ MARIPOSA
(43 miles from the Yosemite Valley):

## Happy Burger
Good inexpensive burgers
5120 Hwy. 140, 209/966-2719

## Charles Street Dinner House
Steaks, seafood, friendly Western theme
209/966-2366

### Savoury's Restaurant

International fusion served in a former CHP office
209/966-7677

### Castillo's Mexican Food

Cantina with generous portions, traditional Mexican dishes
4995 5th St., 209/742-4413

## ❺ LEE VINING

(74 miles from the Yosemite Valley):

### Nicely's Restaurant

Coffee shop style; closed Tuesdays and Wednesdays in winter
Main and 4th Sts., 760/647-6477

### Tioga Gas Mart and Whoa Nellie Deli

Pizza, grilled items, daily special and sandwiches; closed in winter
Hwy. 395 and Hwy. 120W, 760/647-1088

### The Mono Inn

Hearty food and California wines overlooking Mono Lake;
reservations recommended, closed in winter
760/647-6581

## ❻ FISH CAMP

(37 miles from the Yosemite Valley):

### The Narrow Gauge Inn

Rustic and charming, excellent menu;
closed Mondays and Tuesdays and in winter
559/683-6446

### Jackalope's Bar and Grill at the Tenaya Lodge

Traditional American food, burgers, salads, pizzas
559/683-6555

### Sierra Restaurant at the Tenaya Lodge

California cuisine with a rotating menu, but fancier than the Jackalope
888/514-2167

> **Is there anywhere one can get a nice spot of tea?**

Every place has its traditions. At the Ahwahnee Hotel, it's tea and cookies, served every afternoon in the Great Lounge.

It all goes back to Ansel Adams. As a frequent guest of the Ahwahnee, Adams would while away the afternoon hours playing piano in the lounge, attracting the attention of other guests. The hotel staff noticed they had a little audience on their hands, so they decided to serve some tea and cookies to add to the afternoon's entertainment.

Today, hotel guests can sit in the same lounge, sipping on tea and nibbling on cookies in the afternoon as the day winds down. The original piano player is gone, but a gigantic fireplace sets the perfect mood for lounging, reading, and talking to friends in the luxurious setting of the Ahwahnee Hotel.

Where can we pick up picnic supplies?

Yosemite is the ultimate picnic spot. Where you decide to spread your blanket is up to you, but here are your choices for stocking up on the goods. For picnic spots, refer to the map on the next page.

## YOSEMITE VALLEY

The **Village Store** has it all, including a great meat market and fresh produce. It's located at the east end of the Village Mall. **Degnan's Deli,** west of the Village Store next to the post office, provides a good spread of picnic goodies including sandwiches, salads, vegetarian and gourmet foods. **Curry Village Gift and Grocery,** a general store with food and gifts, is located next to the Hamburger Deck at Curry Village. **Housekeeping Camp Store** caters to your picnic needs spring–fall. You can also pick up pre-wrapped picnic items from the **Yosemite Lodge Food Court.**

## SOUTH YOSEMITE

Picnic supplies in south Yosemite can be found at **Pioneer Gift and Groceries** along with film, books and a wide wine selection. **The Pine Tree Market** is in the heart of north Wawona, less than a mile off the main highway on Chilnualna Fall Road.

## NORTH YOSEMITE

There's a limited selection of stores in this area, but the **Crane Flat Gas Station and Store** at the intersection of Big Oat Flat and Tioga Roads provides your basic fare and is open year-round. **Tuolumne Meadows Store** offers the largest selection of picnic supplies in north Yosemite.

**Are there any special seasonal events in Yosemite?**

New Year's Eve, Easter brunch, Thanksgiving dinner—the Ahwahnee Hotel celebrates the holidays with amazing spreads of food and drink and celebrations. One of the classics is the Vintner's Holidays mid-November–mid-December, when master winemakers gather at the Ahwahnee to host a month-long series of banquets, seminars, and wine tastings.

And the Bracebridge Dinner at the Ahwahnee! Every Christmas, the hotel chefs create a seven-course extravaganza, complete with a four-hour colorful Yorkshire Christmas pageant. The tickets are awarded in a lottery system and applications for the following year's dinner should be sent in December 1–January 15. Call 559/253-5604 for more information.

The Ahwahnee follows up with the Chef's Holiday mid-January–February. Talented chefs are on hand to give demonstrations and prepare five-course feasts for participants. Inquire about the Ahwahnee Chef's Package and other events such as a New Year's Eve celebration, Heritige Holidays and Vintner's Holidays (559/253-5636, www.yosemitepark.com/SpecialEventsPackages_EventEvents.aspx).

# V
# Camping and Backpacking

What types of campgrounds are available in Yosemite Valley?

There used to be six campgrounds with 779 campsites nestled between the valley's giant towers of granite. The New Year's flood of 1997 changed that configuration to four campgrounds with 414 campsites, all located at the eastern end of the valley at an elevation of 4,000 feet. When you camp in the valley, don't expect to be hidden away in the forest far away from other campers. These sites are popular and are always the first to go. Most of them operate on a year-round reservation system.

All the campgrounds are listed below, with helpful information, but here's a quick run-down on the valley camps: Check-in and check-out time is 10 A.M. There aren't any recreational vehicle hook-ups, but there are sanitary dumps. Shower facilities are available at Curry Village all year and at Housekeeping Camp starting in mid-April 7 A.M.–10 P.M. Keep in mind that showers are closed 2–3:30 P.M. for cleaning daily. Starting in mid-April, Housekeeping Camp also has a laundromat open 7 A.M.–10 P.M.—quarters only and they do have change machines.

Three of the campgrounds are named after the pine trees that shade the eastern end of the valley. **Lower Pines** offers 60 sites, some near the river. Across the river from Lower Pines sits **North Pines** with 81 sites. **Upper Pines** is the largest of the valley camps with 238 sites and is the only one open all year. All of the Pines' campgrounds offer a sanitary dump station, welcome both RVs and tents, have tap water, nearby showers and are pet-friendly campgrounds. All of the Pines' campsites cost $20 per night with a maximum of six people per site with fire rings, picnic tables, and bear-proof food storage lockers.

Both the **Upper and Lower River** campgrounds were completely washed away in the New Year's flood of 1997.

**Camp 4,** also known as Sunnyside Walk-In Campground, is located across from Yosemite Lodge, serves rock climbers and backpackers. All campers carry in their gear and sleep in communal-type sites. Camp 4 operates on a first-come, first-served basis and costs $5 per person. No pets are allowed.

During the peak months of April–September, reservations are essential and even the first-come, first-served sites often fill by noon May–September.

The recommended campground reservation site is www.recreation.gov or call 877/444-6777. Reservations are no longer available by mail.

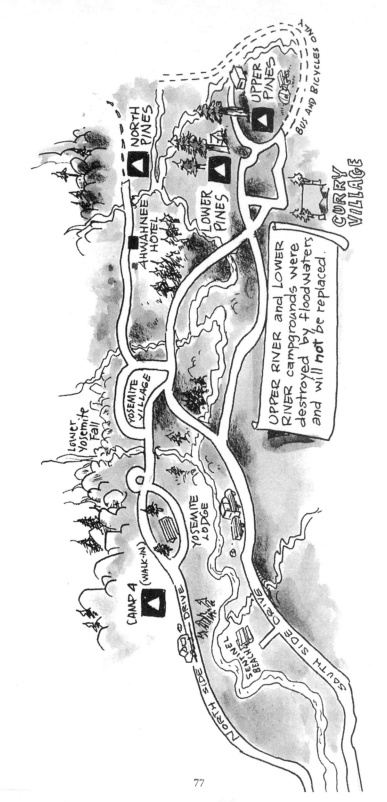

# Campgrounds in Yosemite Valley

| Campground | North Pines | Upper Pines | Lower Pines | Camp 4 Walk-In |
|---|---|---|---|---|
| Elevation (ft.) | 4000 | 4000 | 4000 | 4000 |
| Miles from Yosemite Valley | 0 | 0 | 0 | 0 |
| No. of Sites/Spaces | 68 | 206 | 49 | 35 |
| Daily Fee | $20/s | $20/s | $20/s | $5/p |
| RV Space | • | • | • | |
| Tent Space | • | • | • | • |
| Tap Water | • | • | • | • |
| Flush Toilets | • | • | • | • |
| Pit Toilets | | | | |
| Tables | • | • | • | • |
| Fire Pits or Grill | • | • | • | • |
| Pets Allowed | | • | | |
| Dump Station | | • | | |
| Parking | • | • | • | • |
| Showers Nearby | • | • | • | • |
| Laundry Nearby | • | • | • | • |
| Groceries | • | • | • | • |
| Swimming | • | • | • | • |
| Fishing | • | • | • | • |
| Horseback Riding | • | • | • | • |
| Notes | Open April–October* Reservations required | Open April–November* Reservations required | Open all year Reservations required | Open all year/ walk-in first-come, first-served; Shared campsites; Limited parking available |

* Dates approximate
/s = per site
/p = per person

**What are the campgrounds outside the valley?**

Yosemite Valley may be the heart of the action for visitors, but campers will actually find more campgrounds outside the valley. There are nine total, and even though they're not as busy as the valley camps, they do fill up most summer nights. Arrive early to take advantage of the first-come, first-served system (check-in and check-out time is noon for all campgrounds outside of the valley). A tip for RVs: the only sanitary dumping stations outside the valley are found during the summer at Wawona and Tuolumne Meadows.

## SOUTH YOSEMITE

The **Wawona campground** sits on the banks of the Merced River's South Fork, 25 miles from the valley at an elevation of 4,000 feet. Campsites are open all year, horse camps are open approximately April–October, and if winter is your camping season, prepare for snowy conditions. During the high season, approximately May–September, reservations are required, October–April campsites are first-come, first-served. RVs and tents are welcome, pets are permitted. Eight miles out on Glacier Point Road, you'll come across the **Bridalveil Creek campground.** The elevation here is 7,200 feet, the campground is open approximately July–early September, and pets are permitted in sites other than group and horse camps. Other than group and horse sites, which require reservations, this is a first-come, first-served campground.

Parts of the Wawona and Bridalveil Creek campgrounds are reserved for group use and horse camps only. You'll need to make reservations at www. recreation.gov or call 877/444-6777.

## NORTH YOSEMITE

The park's northern region offers an all-around rougher brand of camping, with higher elevations, smaller campgrounds, and fewer services. **Tuolumne Meadows Campground** is the exception; it's the largest campground in Yosemite with 304 sites, with tons of activities for families, including a horse camp. Half of the sites may be reserved, half are first-come, first-served.

Campers with pets are welcome in most north Yosemite campgrounds, including **Crane Flat Campground,** located at the intersection of Big Oak Flat and Tioga Road, just 17 miles away from the valley. If you're driving in from the west on Highway 120, the first camp you'll see is **Hodgdon Meadow**

**Campground,** which allows pets and mid-April–mid-October and requires reservations. Along the Tioga Road, there are a number of rustic, seasonal campgrounds where you don't need a reservation and where you can really rough it, including **Tamarack Flat, White Wolf, Yosemite Creek,** and **Porcupine Flat.**

## Campgrounds Outside Yosemite Valley

| Campground | Wawona | Bridalveil Creek | Hodgdon Meadow |
|---|---|---|---|
| Location | Hwy. 41 in Wawona | Glacier Point Rd. | Hwy. 120 west near Big Oak Flat Entrance |
| Elevation (ft.) | 4000 | 7200 | 4872 |
| Miles from Yosemite Valley | 27 | 25 | 25 |
| No. of Sites/Spaces | 96 | 110 | 109 |
| Daily Fee | $20/s | $14/s | $20/s |
| RV Space | • | • | • |
| Tent Space | • | • | • |
| Tap Water | • | • | • |
| Stream Water (BOIL) | | | |
| Flush Toilets | • | • | • |
| Pit Toilets | | | |
| Tables | • | • | • |
| Fire Pits or Grill | • | • | • |
| Pets Allowed | • | • | • |
| Dump Station | • | | |
| Parking | • | • | • |
| Showers Nearby | | | |
| Laundry Nearby | • | | • |
| Groceries | • | | |
| Swimming | • | | |
| Fishing | • | • | |
| Horseback Riding | • | | |
| Group Sites | • | • | • |
| Horse Sites | • | • | • |
| Notes | Open all year *First-come, first-served* | Open June–September* *First-come, first-served* | Open all year *Reservations required approx. May–Oct.; First-come, first-served rest of year* |

* Dates approximate
/s = per site

# U.S. FOREST SERVICE CAMPGROUNDS OUTSIDE YOSEMITE

For information on the United States Forest Service campgrounds near Yosemite in the Inyo, Sierra, and Stanislaus National Forests, contact Recreation.gov (877/444-6777, www.recreation.gov).

| Campground | Crane Flat | Tamarack Flat | White Wolf |
|---|---|---|---|
| Location | Hwy. 120 near the Tioga Rd. turnoff | Hwy. 120 east | Hwy. 120 east |
| Elevation (ft.) | 6191 | 6315 | 8000 |
| Miles from Yosemite Valley | 17 | 23 | 31 |
| No. of Sites/Spaces | 166 | 52 | 74 |
| Daily Fee | $20/s | $10/s | $14/s |
| RV Space | • |  | • |
| Tent Space | • | • | • |
| Tap Water | • |  | • |
| Stream Water (BOIL) |  | • |  |
| Flush Toilets | • |  | • |
| Pit Toilets |  | • |  |
| Tables | • | • | • |
| Fire Pits or Grill | • | • | • |
| Pets Allowed | • |  | • |
| Dump Station |  |  |  |
| Parking | • | • | • |
| Showers Nearby |  |  |  |
| Laundry Nearby |  |  |  |
| Groceries | • |  |  |
| Swimming |  |  |  |
| Fishing |  |  | • |
| Horseback Riding |  |  |  |
| Group Sites |  |  |  |
| Horse Sites |  |  |  |
| Notes | Open June–October* Reservations required | Open July–early Sept.* Three-mile access road not suitable for large RVs or trailers | Open July–early Sept.* First-come, first-served |

* Dates approximate
/s = per site

(continued on next page)

# Campgrounds Outside Yosemite Valley (continued)

| Campground | Yosemite Creek | Porcupine Flat | Tuolumne Meadows |
|---|---|---|---|
| Location | Hwy. 20 east | Hwy. 120 east | Hwy. 120 east |
| Elevation (ft.) | 7659 | 8100 | 8600 |
| Miles from Yosemite Valley | 35 | 38 | 55 |
| No. of Sites/Spaces | 40 | 52 | 315 |
| Daily Fee | $10/s | $10/s | $20/s |
| RV Space | | | • |
| Tent Space | • | • | • |
| Tap Water | | | • |
| Stream Water (BOIL) | • | • | |
| Flush Toilets | | | • |
| Pit Toilets | • | • | |
| Tables | • | • | • |
| Fire Pits or Grill | • | • | • |
| Pets Allowed | • | | • |
| Dump Station | | | • |
| Parking | • | • | • |
| Showers Nearby | | | • |
| Laundry Nearby | | | • |
| Groceries | | | • |
| Swimming | | | |
| Fishing | • | | • |
| Horseback Riding | | | • |
| Group Sites | | | • |
| Horse Sites | | | • |
| Notes | Open all year *First-come, first-served* | Open June–September*, *First-come first-served* | Open all year *Reservations required approx. May–Oct.; First-come, first-served rest of year* |

\* Dates approximate
/s = per site

Yosemite has 1,543 campsites and 3.5–4 million visitors each year. Reservations are required for Yosemite Valley's auto campgrounds year-round, and summer–fall for Wawona, Hodgdon Meadow, Crane Flat, and half of Tuolumne Meadows' campgrounds. All other campgrounds are available on a first-come, first-served basis (except for group campgrounds). You can register for vacant campsites starting at 7:30 A.M. with a ranger, or self-register by following the posted instructions. A tip: the campgrounds along Tioga Road are last to fill up.

All reservations can be made through the central reservations system (877/444-6777, www.recreation.gov). Phone reservation hours are 7 A.M.–7 P.M. (PST) November–February and 7 A.M.–9 P.M. (PST) March–October. For the most up-to-date information on booking your campground reservations, visit the National Park Service website for Yosemite (www.nps.gov/yose) and click on camping, or call 209/372-0200.

# Are there any limits or restrictions on camping?

**S**orry, you can't become a full-time resident like our animals in one of the park campgrounds. Thirty days is the limit, and May 1–September 15 you can only camp for a total of two weeks—only seven of those days can be spent in Yosemite Valley and Wawona. At campgrounds that allow them, the maximum length for RVs is 40 feet at Lower and North Pines, 35 feet at all the others except White Wolf where the maximum is 27 feet.

## And now for the rules:

- Camping or sleeping in vehicles is permitted only in designated campsites.
- A maximum of six people (including children) and two vehicles may occupy a campsite.
- Pets are allowed only in specific campgrounds and must be on a leash no longer than six feet at all times. They're not to go on trails or unpaved roads (except the Meadow Loop and Four Mile fire roads in Wawona, on the Carlon Road, and on the Old Big Oak Flat Road between Hodgdon Meadow and Hazel Green Creek) or be left alone at a campsite.
- Quiet hours are 10 P.M.–6 A.M.
- From May 1–October 1, campfires are allowed only 5–10 P.M. in Yosemite Valley. Fires are permitted in out-of-valley campgrounds at any time as long as you are below 9,600 feet in elevation.
  - Generators may be used sparingly 7 A.M.–7 P.M.
  - Wastewater must be disposed of in designated utility drains.
  - Sewage must be disposed of at designated dump stations (Yosemite Valley, Wawona, and Tuolumne Meadows).
  - You must keep your food stored from bears 24 hours a day!
  - Electrical extension cords cannot be connected to restroom outlets.

Well, we got that out of the way. Now let's go camping!

## Can we build a campfire?

The campfire's comforting crackle is one of the best parts of camping, but it has also caused some of our air quality problems and forest fires. As long as you follow a few guidelines, our next generation of campers can enjoy fireside gatherings as well.

Start by using established campfire rings, then check around the area for potential spark hazards. Never leave fires unattended; put them out by stirring in water before you leave the campground, and do a final check for any remaining embers. Remember, during the summer camp season, fires are only allowed 5–10 P.M. in Yosemite Valley. Outside the valley you can have a campfire in the backcountry below 9,600 feet in elevation. The sequoia groves, however, are strict no-fire zones.

If you're using a portable camping stove, refuel it only when it's cold and in a well-ventilated area. Keep any burning charcoals out of tents and vehicles, and douse the coals with water when you're finished—do not allow fires to smoulder.

To fuel your fires, you can bring firewood from home or buy some in the stores both in and out of the valley. Gathering wood is an option outside the valley and sequoia groves, as long as the wood is dead and on the ground. If you try to collect some wood or pine cones in Yosemite Valley or sequoia groves, you might also collect a $50–100 citation.

Not with wet wood!

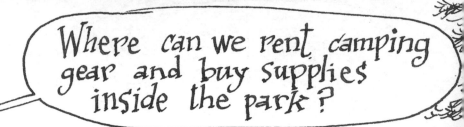

## Where can we rent camping gear and buy supplies inside the park?

**Y**ou're better off renting gear before you arrive in Yosemite. The same equipment will probably cost more in the park, and, frankly, there just isn't much gear to rent here—not even tents. Backpacks ($15.50 per day), sleeping bags ($13 per day) and sleeping pads ($2.50 per day) are sometimes available through the Yosemite Mountaineering School in Curry Village (209/372-8344), but during the summer months most of their equipment is reserved for the school's group trips. Give them a call for current prices and more information. Rentals drop to half price on the third day.

Food, clothing, rock climbing and camping supplies can be purchased in various stores throughout the park.

Wherever you get your camp stuff, here's a short list of essentials: Tent with rainfly, ground cloth, warm sleeping bag, sleeping pad, flashlight, food, cooking stove and fuel, and any personal gear. If you're going to stay at our High Sierra Camps, you might want to pick up travel sheets (13.4 oz.); they're not provided at the camps.

Gimme the works!

YOSEMITE WILDERNESS CT.

## What are the High Sierra camps like?

**H**ikers return year after year to Yosemite's five High Sierra Camps (Glen Aulin, Vogelsang, Merced Lake, Sunrise, and May Lake), located at intervals of 6–10 miles (a day's hike) along a loop trail at elevations of 7,200–10,000 feet. During the months of June–September, each camp offers its own spectacular setting, rustic accommodations, helpful staff, and hearty meals. Unfortunately, youngsters under age seven aren't allowed.

Men and women stay in separate dormitory-style tent cabins, with wood-burning stoves (except at Merced Lake), tables and chairs, candles, and hooks and shelves for gear. Beds are outfitted with mattresses, pillows, woolen blankets or comforters. Sleep-sacks and Trek Towels may be purchased through DNC Parks & Resorts at Yosemite via mail order for confirmed High Camp Guests. They are also available for sale at High Camp stores and the Tuolumne Meadows store. Hikers can even receive the warm welcome of a hot shower, though sometimes usage is limited due to water restrictions.

Breakfasts and dinners are prepared by the camp staff and served in generous portions, and picnic lunches are available upon request. The cost is around $136 plus tax per night for lodging, breakfast, dinner, and showers. Those of you who are camping on your own can opt for dinners and breakfasts only for $35.75 per day, or the box lunch at $10.50.

*Unfortunately... children under seven and bears aren't allowed.*

Due to high demand and limited space, reservations are granted by lottery and you must fill out an application. There are three ways to get an application:

1. Call 559/253-5674 to request an application.

2. Download a pdf of the application at www.yosemitepark.com/ Accomodations_HighSierraCamps.aspx

3. Submit an email request no later than December 31 for the following year. The subject line should read "High Camp Application Request" and be sure to include your name, complete mailing address and your email address. An application will be sent to you.

You can submit a High Sierra Camp lottery application form to Yosemite Reservations no later than January 15 of each year. A maximum of eight spaces (six for meals-only) may be requested on each application form and don't send payment until it is requested. You will be notified by February 28th as to your place in the lottery. All reservations must be paid in full within 30 days of lottery award!

Cancellations are filled by waiting list, then it's telephone inquiry time to fill any other spaces around April 1st, 2008. Open spaces are listed on the Availability page at www.yosemitepark.com/Accomodations_ HighSierraCamps.aspx and are updated weekly. This page is not live until the lottery process is complete. These reservations can only be made by calling the High Sierra Desk at 559/253-5674.

# What is Yosemite's backcountry wilderness like?

"**B**ackcountry" means an area that's reached only by foot or on horseback. In 1984, the U.S. Congress designated almost the entire Yosemite region as wilderness area—all but six percent of it. That means there's plenty of opportunity to lose the crowds and wander into some of the world's most breathtaking scenery.

But don't forget the "wild" part of wilderness; out here, weather and trail conditions can change quickly. At 7,000–11,000 feet, your dusty trail can turn into a snow-covered path faster than you can say, "Did we pack our snow shoes?" During spring and early summer, winter's runoff can fill the rivers and streams to dangerous levels. Any crossing, with or without a bridge, should be taken with caution.

Hiking the backcountry in fall is like walking under a waterfall of autumn color. Expect freezing temperatures at night, and be prepared for sudden storms.

Winter's white cover doesn't mean the backcountry is off limits, it just means you have to trade in your boots for cross-country skis or snowshoes. Both groomed and ungroomed trails cross expanses of wilderness to places like Glacier Point, Crane Flat, and the south rim of the valley. Be sure to call ahead for trail conditions.

## Here's a sampling of what you'll find in the park's backcountry regions:

- The canyons in the northern and western regions of Yosemite contain some of the most beautiful country in the Sierra Nevada.

- The Hetch Hetchy area between Highway 120 and the Tuolumne River hosts a large variety of elevations and plant life. One of the more popular trails here rises more than 10,000 feet to the summit of Mt. Hoffman.

- Tuolumne Meadows trails (north of Highway 120) wind through a subalpine world of jagged peaks, crystal-clear lakes, glaciated domes, and roaring cascades. The sights here match any visitor's greatest expectations.

- The Tuolumne Meadows trails south and east of Highway 120 are used frequently, so reserve your space with a wilderness permit before you embark. They're popular for good reason: these paths take you past spectacular passes and mountain lakes.

- Yosemite Valley is a safe option, providing a rich array of history and scenery on many different trails.

- Glacier Point offers cooler temperatures than you'll find in Wawona or Yosemite Valley, with elevations ranging between 6,000–7,000 feet. There are fewer and less-used trails here, with amazing views, that take you to the edge of Yosemite Valley or on longer excursions through a variety of mountain life zones.

- Yosemite's southeastern backcountry has the highest trail point in the entire park, and the journey there is filled with green havens of lodgepole pines and unique, subalpine regions.

# Are there any organized hiking trips into Yosemite's wilderness?

**O**ne of the best ways to see our backcountry is on a seven-day or five-day hike led by National Park Service naturalist rangers. The trips are day-hikes between the High Sierra Camps and include dormitory style accommodations and meals. You need to be in good shape for these treks, as they can cover up to 10 miles each day and climb up to over 10,000 feet at some locations—you'll be carrying your own snacks, clothing, water for the trail and sheets or sleep sacks. Before starting the journey, you should spend a day around Tuolumne Meadows to acclimate to the higher elevations.

The price (subject to change) is approximately $1,159 per person for six nights' lodging/$825 for four nights' lodging and all meals at the High Sierra Camps. Weather permitting, the hikes usually depart two days a week, early July–early September. Children under age 12 are not permitted, and anyone under age 18 must be accompanied by an adult. For more information and reservations, call the High Sierra desk (559/253-5674). You can also check out the Yosemite Association's Field Seminar Program (www.yosemite.org/seminars/index.html). Yosemite Mountaineering School (209/372-8344) also offers a guided backpacking and day hike programs during the summer.

You may want to explore the backcountry on horseback or by hiking next to a pack animal. These trips require a minimum of three pack and/or saddle animals, and each group must be accompanied by a guide. Mid July–early September, four-day trips depart on Saturdays (southbound) and Wednesdays (northbound); six-day trips depart every Sunday, mid July–late August, visiting the five High Camps for one night each. Children must be at least seven years old and 44 inches tall. Weight limits are no more than 150 pounds per pack animal and 225 pounds per saddle animal. For more information about guided saddle trips call the High Sierra desk (559/253-5674).

*A little less organized please.*

# When and why do we need wilderness permits?

**P**ermits are required for overnight stays in the Yosemite's backcountry. No problem—they're free, and they cut down on overcrowding during peak season by limiting the number of campers in the areas. During the winter, permits provide important safety information and also help rangers keep track of whoever is exploring around the area. Permits are not required for day hikes.

Of these free permits, 40 percent are available on a first-come basis the day of or 24 hours before your trip. You can complete the task in person at the following permit stations: Yosemite Valley Wilderness Center located in Yosemite Village between the Post Office and the Ansel Adams Gallery (summer only; register at visitor center in winter), Wawona Wilderness Center located in Hill's Studio just to the left of the Wawona Hotel (summer only; self-registration during winter), Big Oak Flat on the Big Oak Flat Road (Highway 120) at the park entrance (summer only; self-registration during winter), Badger Pass ranger station A-frame at Badger Pass on Glacier Point Road (winter only), Hetch Hetchy entrance station (open limited hours), and Tuolumne Meadows Wilderness Permit Station located in parking lot 0.25 mile from the Tuolumne Meadows Ranger Station (summer only; self-registration during winter at ski hut). Call 209/372-0200 for open permit station locations and hours.

To reserve your wilderness permit by mail send a reservation request letter to Yosemite Association, P.O. Box 545, Yosemite, CA 95389. Be sure to include your name, address, daytime phone, number of people in your party,

I said... WE COME UP HERE TO GET AWAY FROM EVERYONE!!

method of travel (foot, ski, snowshoe, horse, etc.), number of stock (if applicable), start and end dates, entry and exit trailheads and principle destination. Making a request does *not* guarantee a reservation. If your requested trailhead and dates are available, you will receive a confirmation letter in the mail. If your reservation request is made less than two days or more than 24 weeks in advance, it will be rejected *without notice.* Be sure to include a $5 non-refundable processing fee per person or list your credit card information. Checks may be made payable to the Yosemite Association. Requests will be processed 2–24 weeks in advance of the first day of your trip.

You can reserve by phone or go online to to make a reservation (209/372-0740, Mon.–Fri. 8:30 A.M.–4:30 P.M. PST, www.nps.gov/yose/wilderness).

## What should we know about camping and backpacking in Yosemite's backcountry?

A wilderness excursion is a bit different than a stroll through Yosemite Village. Hiking the backcountry requires an ample amount of time for rest and searching for that perfect campsite. Park regulations say you must be four trail miles from Yosemite Valley, Tuolumne Meadows, Glacier Point, Hetch Hetchy or at least one trail mile from any road while camping, and in groups of no more than 15 people on the trails and eight for more than 0.25 mile off-trail hikes. Our wilderness area is a wildlife preserve with over 800 miles of trails; that means no pets, weapons, bicycles, or strollers. You can stay a maximum of 30 days in the backcountry, and it's a good idea to let friends and family know your itinerary.

### Here are a few rules of thumb to remember:

- Be extra careful crossing streams during spring runoff.
- Be sure to take a guide or topographic map—these are for sale in park stores, the visitor center and at the Wilderness Center is Yosemite Valley.
- Pack out all trash.
- Travel and camp on durable surfaces.
- Be considerate of other visitors.
- Use gas stoves instead of firewood.
- Protect yourself and the wildlife by using proper food storage containers. Bear canisters are required in most of Yosemite's wilderness!
- Choose existing, well-used campsites at least 100 feet from water.
- Be sure to check trail conditions and weather before departing.
- Bring a first-aid kit and know how to use it.
- Purify all drinking water by boiling 3–5 minutes, with Giardia-rated filters, or with iodine-based chemical treatment.
- Protect water quality by disposing human waste in small holes at least 100 feet from water and by doing all washing at similar distances from water.

Abiding by these rules will enhance your backcountry experience and help preserve Yosemite's natural heritage. For current trail conditions, visit www.nps.gov/archive/yose/wilderness/trailconditions.htm.

## Bear Facts and Amazing Bear Tricks

- The last Grizzly bear was killed in Yosemite in 1895 at Crescent Lake. The black bear is the only species left in the park.

- Yosemite's black bears can be a variety of colors including brown, blonde, cinnamon, or black.

- Yosemite black bears typically range in size 150-400 pounds. The largest bear ever measured in Yosemite tipped the scales at 690 pounds. These are omnivores and will eat almost anything including insects, small rodents, berries, acorns, seeds, and human food.

- It is estimated that there are 300-500 black bears living within the borders of Yosemite National Park.

- Many of the black bears go into a den in the winter months for a sleep that is not a true hibernation. The young cubs are born in late winter and come out of the den in spring to forage for food with their mother.

- Bears in Yosemite have figured out how to get garbage out of "bear-proof" dumpsters by laying down on the hinged top door, causing it to close. Then by keeping one leg outside, they hang upside down inside the dumpster, grab the garbage, and pull themselves back out.

- Bears have figured out several ways to get the food bags that campers hang from trees. A sow will sometimes send one of her cubs up the tree after the food, and some bears will actually chew through the tree limbs to send the food crashing down.

- Some trees have wires between them for hanging food. Bears have been known to shinny out to the middle of the wire, with their weight bending it toward the ground. Then they let go, sling-shooting the food some distance away. All that's left to do is hunt for the food where it landed.

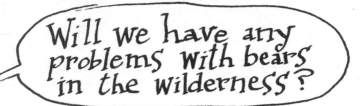

# Will we have any problems with bears in the wilderness?

**B**lack bears are curious creatures, and sometimes they will rummage around populated areas in search of accessible food. They've been known to rip open car doors in search of goodies and even freefall from branches to snag the food bags that campers hang from trees. Both people and bears have been injured and repeat offender bears have been killed as a result. You can help save people and bears by following some simple suggestions.

Due to a Federal law regarding food storage, visitors may no longer store food in their cars at night! Bears can smell food inside and will break in to get it—even in the trunk! Failure to store your food properly may result in impoundment of your food, car, revocation of your camping permit or even a fine of up to $5,000!

Food lockers are available at ALL of the park campgrounds, at trailheads, in the Curry Village parking lots, and at several lodging accommodations. Use them for your sake *and* the bears' sake!

Store all food, including supplies like ice chests and cans, in lockers where provided, and use clips to secure these boxes. Any grocery bags, garbage, and other scented items like soap, sunscreen, and toothpaste should be stored as well. Airtight containers will supply that extra bit of prevention.

Food should be stored day and night. Bears have been known to take midday strolls through campgrounds and picnic areas.

Keep your campsite clean by putting trash in bear-proof canisters, lockers and dumpsters. While you're out on day hikes, store all food supplies at the trailhead, either in your car trunk or in lockers, or keep it with you at all times while hiking.

Don't leave your backpack lying around. Bears think packs are gift-wrapped food.

In the backcountry, plan ahead to store your food by renting ($3 per trip) or buying ($75) bear-proof food canisters, available at the Curry Village and Tuolumne Meadows Mountain Shop, Tuolumne Store, the Village Sport Shop, Crane Flat Grocery, the Wawona Store, Wawona Information Station, Tuolumne Meadows Grocery, and wilderness centers throughout the park and at the Hetch Hetchy Entrance Station. Or visit the Yosemite Association's store at www.yosemitestore.com to purchase.

If you're staying in hard-sided cabins or rooms, keep your supplies indoors and keep the windows closed. In canvas tent-cabins, all food-like bear magnets must be kept in lockers or bear-proof containers.

With all these precautions, you might have already figured out the most important one: never approach a bear, especially cubs. There are approximately four hundred bears in the 1,200 miles of Yosemite, and if you come across one of them, clap your hands, yell, bang pots together, whatever you can do to seem bigger and badder. After any bear encounter, report it to the nearest ranger. One more hint: if a bear already has your backpack in its paws, let it go, because hey, that backpack is gone.

# Rock Climbing in Yosemite: Feats and Facts

Almost every technique and piece of equipment used by rock climbers around the world was either developed or perfected at Yosemite National Park, such as:

- 1940s–1960s – Stove leg pitons (actual legs from stoves) were first used and later refined during ascents of El Capitan.

- 1950s–1980s – The big wall technique was developed here and used in the first ascent of El Capitan in 1958 and other subsequent Yosemite climbs.

- 1970s–1980s – The use and development of artificial nuts and wedges made of aluminum in Yosemite has contributed to a new "clean climbing" ethic in the sport.

- 1980s–present – The use of spring-loaded cams and other mechanical protection devices was refined at Yosemite.

- The development and refinement of crack-climbing techniques has allowed climbers to scale 5.12 cracks in Yosemite.

- Some of the sport's most noteworthy free-soloing climbs have taken place in Yosemite including "Astroman" on Washington Column and "The Rostrum" in the Merced River Canyon.

- Sunnyside Walk-in Campground was renamed Camp Four and in February of 2003 was listed in the National Register of Historic Places for "its significant association with the growth and development of rock climbing in the Yosemite Valley during the 'golden years' of pioneer mountaineering."

- Camp Four has some of the most famous and most difficult "boulder problems" (short climbs of 30 feet or less without ropes) in the world, including "Midnight Lighting" and "Thriller."

- It was in the parking lot of Camp Four that Patagonia founder, Yvon Chouinard, first began his outdoor equipment legacy by creating and selling climbing gear.

# VI
# Recreational Opportunities

## What's there to do around here?

**W**hen you first enter Yosemite, you're sure to be overwhelmed by how big it is. You'll wish you had wings so you could take it all in. Well, there are plenty of year-round activities that allow you to experience the best the park has to offer.

A journey on our 800 miles of walking trails begins with a single step. From steep, lofty hikes to mellow strolls on the valley floor, these many paths take you through Yosemite's most spectacular landscapes.

For a swifter route, we have 12 miles of bike trails winding through the valley. Weather permitting, you can rent bikes year-round and pedal your way past meadows and along the river to famous vistas of Half Dome and El Capitan—but stick to the paved bike trails and roads.

After a hot summer day on the trails, a great way to cool down is to take a plunge into cool waters. There are plenty of good swimming holes along the sandy beaches of the Merced River at the eastern end of the valley, or higher up among the lakes, creeks, and rivers of northern Yosemite; but be careful of the chilly, swift currents. You could also try the calmer waters in the swimming pools at Yosemite Lodge, Curry Village, or as a guest at the Ahwahnee or Wawona Hotels.

In the summer, rafting the Merced River is a fun and relaxing way to explore the valley. If sailing is your choice, the afternoon winds on Tenaya Lake provide the perfect fuel for sailboats and windsurfers (motor boats not permitted).

You don't have to go far to cast a line in Yosemite waters: we have 770 miles of rivers and streams and 127 lakes and reservoirs.

On horseback, you can tour the valley and high country (summers only), trying the same mode of travel as Yosemite's native peoples and pioneers.

After watching rock climbers tackle the challenging granite faces, you might be tempted to give it a shot yourself. The Yosemite Mountaineering School is one of the best at teaching basic technique and proper equipment use. The school also offers intermediate and advanced lessons.

Some people might ask, "Why ruin a perfectly nice walk in the park?" But we do have a great nine-hole golf course next to the Wawona Hotel.

One of the park's best-kept secrets is the wide range of activities found in winter. That's when you can downhill ski at Badger Pass, ice-skate at Curry Village, cross-country ski some of our 90 miles of trails, or take a ranger-led snowshoe tour. Educational and recreational activities are also available through the Yosemite Association's programs.

The entire park is accessible to hikers, but unless you have the survival instincts of a bear, you have to be an expert with a map and compass to travel off-trail. When you hike the trails in Yosemite, you're carrying on a tradition that goes back hundreds, even thousands, of years. These trails—trekked by Native Americans, pioneers, and generations of backpackers and hikers—are your best shot at getting an insider's look at Yosemite.

## Yosemite Valley

You can cover much of Yosemite Valley with easy hikes to Mirror Lake, Vernal Fall Bridge and Lower Yosemite Fall and with tougher treks to the valley's rim via Yosemite Falls Trail, the Four-Mile Trail (summer), Snow Creek Trail, and the Vernal and Nevada Falls Trail (summer). Any one you choose will provide spectacular vistas of the area. As rewarding as the demanding trail to the summit of Half Dome can be, plan this trip sometime between late May–early October only.

## South Yosemite

Wawona is the starting point for many great hikes, and it's less crowded than the valley. You can start with the easy route along Meadow Loop, then try the tougher Chilnualna Fall trail or the hike to Mariposa Big Trees (or, consider taking the free shuttle from Wawona to the Mariposa Grove and walking *downhill* to Wawona!). Once you're in the Mariposa Grove, try the easy walks to the Grizzly Giant or Wawona Point. Higher up are the trails starting from Glacier Point Road, including the popular Panorama and Pohona Trails and the short hikes to Taft Point, Sentinel Dome, and Mono Meadow. For wilderness excursions, the Glacier Point Road trails lead to the Clark Range and the southern portion of the park.

## North Yosemite

Hetch Hetchy reservoir, located in the northwest part of the park, is at the same elevation as the valley, but it's usually much warmer. In winter, this is a good starting point for day hikes such as the main trail from the reservoir at the top of the dam, which will take you past some awesome falls. Summer and fall are the times to tackle the trails along Tioga Road, including the easy hike to Tuolomne Meadows, the moderate hikes to Harden and Lukens Lakes, and the challenging 13-mile hike down to the valley, or the tough treks up to North Dome, May and Gaylor Lakes, and Mono Pass. The high country trails around Tuolumne Meadows offer cooler temperatures and smaller crowds. From here, eight different trailheads lead backpackers and day hikers into a range of wilderness adventures.

## Fire Facts

- Between 1931 and 1996, there were over 2,700 natural fires caused by lightning in Yosemite, an average of 43 natural fires a year.

- Since 1972, natural fires have burned an average of 2,400 acres a year in Yosemite's wilderness.

- Since 1970, staff-controlled prescribed burns have torched an average of 1,300 acres a year in Yosemite's lower elevations.

- If you see smoke while you're in the park it could be from a prescribed fire set by National Park Service rangers under proper conditions. This helps keep the park's forests and meadows ecologically healthy and to restore natural conditions. These fires are allowed to burn without intervention in areas full of dead and down fuel – and where there's no threat to property or human lives. Boundaries are set and fire fighters are on hand to assure that the fire remains controlled.

# What should we take on our day hike?

You won't get far without a sturdy pair of sneakers or boots, and you'll wish you hadn't gone so far if the weather changes and you're caught without an extra layer of clothing and a rainproof shell. Sometimes a hike lasts longer than you expect; instead of having to find your way back in the dark, pack a flashlight.

Plenty of water is essential, especially in hot weather and on difficult hikes. It's a good idea to bring snacks, particularly with children along. Once kids become hungry and thirsty, it doesn't matter how blue the lake is or how colorful the wildflowers are, they want to go home. Some favorite snacks for hikers of all ages are granola bars, popcorn, dried and fresh fruit, and trail mix. Whatever you bring, remember to pack out your trash.

Once you're away from the visitor areas, your only bathroom convenience is the toilet paper you carry with you. Human waste must be buried at least six inches deep, 100 feet or more from any water and trails.

A compact first-aid kit or even a few bandages will take care of any cuts and scrapes. Before you embark on your hikes, you'd be smart to apply lip balm, insect repellent, a hat and sunscreen.

Depending on your interests, you can bring other items along that will make your adventures more interesting, such as field books, binoculars, a camera, and fishing gear. If you plan on going off-trail, a map and compass and the know-how to use them are vital tools.

I keep thinking we forgot something

# Where can we hike in the valley and escape the crowds?

**B**elieve it or not, there are places to hike in the valley where you won't be one of thousands of people. They're not exactly secret spots, but they're less crowded than are most popular hikes to Happy Isles, the Vernal Fall Bridge, Nevada Fall's brink, and the bases of Yosemite and Bridalveil Fall. In winter, even these hot spots are uncrowded, and with the valley's lower elevation, you won't need a pair of snowshoes to get around. In the first month of spring, the waterfalls are gushing but the people-traffic is only a trickle (except on weekends). Same goes for the fall, when smaller audiences get to see the brilliant show of changing colors.

Then there's late spring and summer, when flash floods of visitors roar into the valley. If you want to avoid being swept away, there are some options. While most visitors are near the visitor facilities to the east of Yosemite Lodge, you can head west to escape the crowds and wander through some of the valley's best scenery. Most of these trails are level hikes, which lead along the Merced River, past forests, meadows, and wildflower havens. I suggest the Sentinel/Cook's Meadow (7.5 miles) and the El Capitan/Pohono Bridge/Bridalveil (six miles) loop trails.

One last tip: weekdays and early mornings are less crowded hiking times in every season.

*We'd like an easy day hike. Any suggestions?*

If you're looking for an easy trail that takes no more than 2.5–3 hours, the following chart will give you some suggestions. These popular hikes follow along flat trails that won't wipe you out for the rest of the day. The trailheads are easy to find, with scenic photo spots of famous sights, picnic areas, and plenty of ways to hop onto other good trails. All of them are good hikes for families with children, and some have the added bonus of a place to swim and fish. Be prepared for lots of company on these routes, as many visitors will be following the same paths.

| HIKE | TIME | DISTANCE | DIFFICULTY | STARTS FROM |
|---|---|---|---|---|
| **Yosemite Valley** | | | | |
| Bridalveil Fall | 20 min. rt | 0.5 mile | easy | Bridalveil Fall lot |
| Camp Curry Loop | 2 hrs. | 2.8 miles | easy | Camp Curry |
| Happy Isles | 20 min. rt | 0.5 mile | easy | Happy Isles |
| Lower Yosemite Fall | 20 min. rt | 0.5 mile | easy | Yosemite Falls lot |
| Mirror Lake/Meadow | 1 hr. rt to lake | 1.0 mile | easy | Mirror Lake shuttle stop |
| | 2 hrs. loop | 3.0 miles | easy | Mirror Lake shuttle stop |
| Vernal Fall Bridge | 1 hr. rt | 0.8 mile | easy | Happy Isles |
| Yosemite Valley Loop | 2 hrs. | 2.8 miles | easy | Sentinel Bridge lot |
| Yosemite Village Loop | 2 hrs. | 3.3 miles | easy | Yosemite Falls lot |
| **South Yosemite** | | | | |
| Grizzly Giant | 1 hr. rt | 0.8 mile | easy | Mariposa Grove |
| Sentinel Dome | 2 hrs. rt | 2.2 miles | easy | Glacier Point Road |
| Taft Point | 2 hrs. rt | 2.2 miles | easy | Glacier Point Road |
| Wawona Meadow Loop | 2.5 hrs. | 3.0 miles | easy | Wawona |
| Wawona Point | 45 min. rt | 1.0 mile | easy | Mariposa Grove |
| **North Yosemite** | | | | |
| Pothole Dome | 1 hr. rt | 0.5 mile | easy | Tuolumne Meadows |
| Soda Springs | 1 hr. rt | 1.5 miles | easy | Tuolumne Meadows |
| Tenaya Lake Loop | 2 hrs. | 3.1 miles | easy | Highway 120 |
| Tuolumne Meadows | 1 hr. rt | 1.5 miles | easy | Tioga Road |

**Note:**

rt = round-trip

## How about some more challenging hikes?

**T**hese trails are a bit tougher than the easy hikes, requiring more time and a little more oomph to walk up some moderate slopes and occasional steep parts. Families with children are welcome to have a go; just make sure you have plenty of water and snacks. Many of these treks will lead you to great picnicking spots, awesome scenery, historic buildings, and lakes to fish and swim in during the summer months.

| HIKE | TIME | DISTANCE | DIFFICULTY | STARTS FROM |
|------|------|----------|------------|-------------|
| **Yosemite Valley** | | | | |
| Mirror Lake Loop | 4 hrs. | 4.8 miles | moderate | Mirror Lake shuttle stop |
| Tenaya Canyon Loop | 4-6 hrs. | 6.6 miles | moderate | Valley stables |
| Vernal Fall (top) | 3-4 hrs. rt | 4.6 miles | moderate + | Happy Isles |
| West Valley Loop | 3.5 hrs. | 4.0 miles | moderate | Devil's Elbow picnic area |
| **South Yosemite** | | | | |
| Dewey Point | 4-6 hrs. rt | 7.0 miles | moderate | Glacier Point Road |
| Four Mile Trail to Yosemite Valley | 3-4 hrs. | 4.5 miles | moderate | Glacier Point Road |
| Mariposa Grove | 4-5 hrs. rt | 6.3 miles | moderate | Mariposa Grove |
| McGurk's Meadow and Bridalveil Creek | 3.5 hrs. rt | 4.0 miles | moderate | Glacier Point Road |
| Mono Meadow and Mount Starr King View | 3 hrs. rt | 3.0 miles | moderate | Glacier Point Road |
| Wawona Tunnel Tree down to Mariposa Grove | 2-3 hrs. | 2.5 miles | moderate | Mariposa Grove |
| **North Yosemite** | | | | |
| Cascade Creek | 3.5 hrs. rt | 5.0 miles | moderate | Tioga Road |
| Dog Lake | 4 hrs. rt | 3.0 miles | moderate | Tuolumne Meadows |
| Elizabeth Lake | 3.5 hrs. rt | 4.6 miles | moderate + | Tioga Road |
| Harden Lake | 4 hrs. rt | 5.0 miles | moderate | White Wolf |
| Lembert Dome | 3 hrs. rt | 2.8 miles | moderate + | Tioga Road |
| Lukens Lake I | 3 hrs. rt | 4.6 miles | moderate | White Wolf |
| Lukens Lake II | 1 hr. rt | 1.6 miles | moderate | Tioga Road |
| Lyell Canyon | 4 hrs. + rt | 6-14 miles | moderate | Tioga Road |
| May Lake | 2 hrs. rt | 2.4 miles | moderate | Tioga Road |
| Merced Grove of Sequoia | 3 hrs. rt | 4.0 miles | moderate | Big Oak Flat |
| Wapama Falls | 3.5 hrs. rt | 4.0 miles | moderate | Evergreen |

**Note:**

rt = round-trip

+ = more difficult/more time

# What are some great butt-kicking hikes?

For those who like to get their hearts really pumping and feel the burn in their legs, here's a list of some wilderness and high country trails that will happily oblige. You'll need to be in good shape and carefully plan your trip for these babies, but they'll pay you back with great scenery, fewer crowds, and a feeling of accomplishment once you've finished. Most of these can be done in a day, but many of them also have overnight camping areas along the way. Just be sure you have the time and energy before embarking on these journeys, as most of them have strenuous uphill climbs on switchback trails, and the higher elevations mean that much more huffing and puffing.

ARE YOU **SURE** YOU WANT TO DO THIS?

| HIKE | TIME | DISTANCE | DIFFICULTY | STARTS FROM |
|---|---|---|---|---|
| **Yosemite Valley** | | | | |
| Four Mile Trail to Glacier Point | 6-8 hrs. rt | 9.6 miles | strenuous ++ | Southside Drive |
| Half Dome | 10-12 hrs rt | 16.4 miles | strenuous | Happy Isles |
| Tenaya Canyon/Snow Creek Trail to North Dome | 8-10 hrs. rt | 19.2 miles | strenuous ++ | Mirror Lake |
| Vernal and Nevada Falls | 4-6 hrs. rt | 5.9 miles | strenuous | Happy Isles |
| Yosemite Falls | 6-8 hrs. rt | 7.0 miles | strenuous | Yosemite Falls lot |
| **South Yosemite** | | | | |
| Chilnualna Fall | 6-8 hrs. rt | 8.0 miles | strenuous | Wawona |
| Panorama Trail to Yosemite Valley | 6-8 hrs. | 8.5 miles | strenuous - | Glacier Point |
| Wawona Hotel to Mariposa Big Trees | 8-10 hrs. rt | 13.0 miles | strenuous - | Mariposa Grove |
| **North Yosemite** | | | | |
| Cathedral Lakes | 4-6 hrs. rt | 7.9 miles | strenuous + | Tuolumne Meadows |
| Gaylor Lakes | 3 hrs. rt | 3.0 miles | strenuous | Tioga Road |
| Glen Aulin and Waterwheel Falls | 8-10 hrs. rt | 14.0 miles | strenuous ++ | Tuolumne Meadows |
| May Lake to Mount Hoffmann | 6-8 hrs. rt | 6.0 miles | strenuous | Old Tioga Road |
| Monc Pass | 4-6 hrs. rt | 4.0 miles | strenuous | Tioga Road |
| North Dome | 6-8 hrs. rt | 9.6 miles | strenuous - | Tioga Road |
| Yosemite Creek to Yosemite Valley | 8 hrs. | 13 miles | strenuous | Tioga Road |

**Note:**

rt = round-trip

+ = more difficult/more time

++ = very strenuous

- = less strenuous

# Can we mountain bike in Yosemite?

CHECK OUT THE VIEW!

The good news for mountain bikers is that you are allowed on the public roads as well as more than 12 miles of biking trails winding through the valley's best scenery. The bad news is, that's it; all hiking trails and meadows are off-limits to two-wheelers. The Glacier Point and Tioga Roads are open to bikers in the summer, as are some roads in Wawona. If you want to ride off-trail, try some of the dirt roads and trails in the National Forest areas outside the park.

Off-trail riding is barred in Yosemite to protect the vegetation, wildlife, and hikers. Some road use is limited as well, like the paved paths to Mirror Lake and Yosemite Falls, to prevent any collisions with the many folks strolling along.

With the valley's heavy car traffic in summer and early fall, it's a safe bet to keep off the main valley roads with your bike. Try the valley's east end bike paths, where there are no cars and fewer crowds.

## A Few Guidelines before You Hit the Road

- You must stay in the valley on flat, paved surfaces.
- Riders under the age of 18 are required to wear helmets, which are included in the cost of your rental bicycle.
- Obey all traffic laws and park signs.
- Alert pedestrians when passing.
- One rider per bike – carry no passengers.
- Ride single-file on the right hand side of the road or path.
- Rental bikes are not allowed on Mirror Lake Hill and Lower Yosemite Fall Trail because of steep inclines and predictable pedestrian traffic.

# Can we rent bikes?

With 12 miles of paved trails and access to all the roads biking is a great way to see the valley. Beach cruisers are available all year at Yosemite Lodge (unless it's snowing, raining, or just too cold to pedal) and at Curry Village during the summer. You can rent bikes by the hour or day, and they'll throw in helmets and locks, free of charge. Child trailers are available. Bikes can't be reserved, but don't worry, they never run out of them.

Bikes rent for $7.50 per hour, so if you plan on riding around for four hours or more, you might as well have the bike all day for $24.50. If you choose a bike with an attached trailer for the kids you are looking at an hourly rate of $13.50 and a daily rate of $42. If you're up for a shorter tour, you can roam all of the bike paths in a couple of hours or less.

The rental shop is located next to the swimming pool at Yosemite Lodge (shuttle stop #8)—call the shop at 209/372-1208 for more information. The Curry Village Recreation Center (shuttle stop #13 or #21) is next to the hamburger stand and can be reached at 209/372-8319. The rental locations are open daily spring through fall; call the shops or check your *Yosemite Today* for current hours. In 2004 36,852 bicycles were rented in Yosemite Valley!

## Where can we ski in the park?

No other ski resort in the entire state can make the same claim as Yosemite Park: We have California's first ski area, Badger Pass. This granddaddy of the slopes has been going strong since 1935, and over the years, generations of skiers have learned to downhill, cross-country, and, more recently, snowboard on its friendly terrain. Badger Pass (209/372-8430, www.yosemitepark.com/BadgerPass.aspx) offers a triple-chair lift, three double-chairs, one cable tow lift, 10 ski runs, and 90 miles of cross-country trails and 25 miles of machine-groomed track through some of the best scenery in the world.

Downhill skiers and snowboarders can receive expert instruction from the Badger Pass Ski School as well as rent all the necessary equipment at the local ski shop. For all-day rentals of downhill skis, boots, and poles, it costs $24 for adults and $19 for children, ages twelve and under. Snowboards and boots run $35 for all-day rentals for adults and $29.50 for kids. The Guaranteed Learn to Ski package runs $59 for adults and $49 for kids—the same package for snowboarding will run $69 and $59. Lift tickets run $38 for adults full day and $28 for a half day; juniors are $32 for a full-day and $22 for a half day; children's tickets run $15 for a full-day and $11 for a half-day. If you are a senior you are in luck—you get to ski free mid-week and non-holidays otherwise it will be $32 for a full-day on weekends and holidays, $22 for a half-day. Season passes are available too—$376 for adults and juniors, $118 for kids 12 and under.

Cross-country skiers receive the same services without having to pay trail fees. Skis, boots, and poles go for $21.50 for adults, $20 for juniors (13–17 years old) and $11.50 for kids (12 and under)—half-day rates are also available. The Learn to Ski package runs $31, including

Well... it *is* called Badger Pass.

WOOOSH!

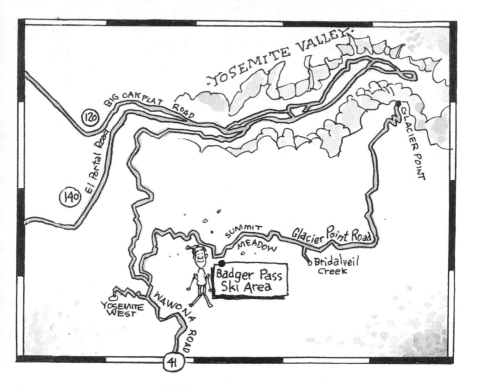

equipment rental. Additional guided cross-country adventures take you to Glacier Point for an overnight, snow camping, trans-Sierra ski tour or the Tuolumne Meadows Hut tour. Prices begin at $160 per night per person—call the Yosemite Mountaineering School and Guide Service (209/372-8444) for information and reservations.

Special Badger Pass ski packages offer special deals including all winter access passes, mid-week lift ticket deals, early bird season passes and ski and stay packages.

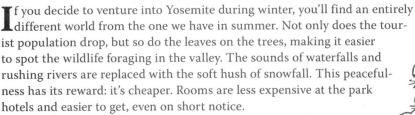

# What else is there to do in the winter besides ski?

**I**f you decide to venture into Yosemite during winter, you'll find an entirely different world from the one we have in summer. Not only does the tourist population drop, but so do the leaves on the trees, making it easier to spot the wildlife foraging in the valley. The sounds of waterfalls and rushing rivers are replaced with the soft hush of snowfall. This peacefulness has its reward: it's cheaper. Rooms are less expensive at the park hotels and easier to get, even on short notice.

Curry Village opens its outdoor ice rink mid-November–mid-March. The best things about winter in the park are all the special seasonal activities. The two-hour skating sessions begin at 3:30 P.M. and end at 9:30 P.M. during the week, weekends and holidays they start at 8:30 A.M. Keep in mind there is an hour between sessions for ice cleaning. You can enjoy the views of Half Dome and Glacier Point while skating under a starry sky, or sit beside a crackling fire drinking hot chocolate in the outdoor fire ring ($8 for adults and $6 for children under age 12). Skate rentals are $3 for both adults and kids, and the starry sky is free. For more information, call 209/372-8319.

Once the snow starts falling, kids of all ages think of one thing: play time! To get your dose of fun, head for the slippery slopes near Crane Flat Campground and the Tioga Road juncture, or just south of the park on Highway 41 at Goat Meadow in the Sierra National Forest. Both are great areas for sledding, tobogganing, and snow tubing. If you are in Badger Pass, you can rent a tube at the Yosemite Tubing Area—each two-hour session costs $11 per person.

Sessions run 11:30 A.M.–1:30 P.M. and 2 P.M.–4 P.M. Call 209/372-8444 for current conditions and session availability.

If you have a pair of snowshoes, you can hike around on your own on some snow-covered terrain, like that at Badger Pass, Crane Flat, and the Mariposa Big Trees. There are also two-hour ranger-led walks (snowshoes provided) departing every day of the winter from Badger Pass ranger station with a suggested donation of $5. Snowshoes and boots are available to rent at the Cross-Country Ski School at Badger Pass and the Crane Flat Gas Station for $19.50 per day and $16.50 for a half-day for both adults and children.

Some of you might prefer the warmth of an enclosed motor coach in which you can take a two-hour narrated tour of the park (209/372-4386 for reservations, www.yosemitepark.com/Activities_GuidedBusTours.aspx, $22 for adults, $18 for seniors, $11.50 for children over five). The tour starts at Yosemite Lodge at the Falls (shuttle stop #8) and operates year-round. You may also stop by the Yosemite Lodge Tour and Activity Desk, Curry Village Tour and Activity Desk or the Village Area Tour and Activity Desk for tour information.

# Where can we swim in the park?

**O**ur streams and lakes may be a little on the chilly side, but after roaming around on a hot day, I wouldn't have it any other way. Before I tell you about some good swimming holes, you should learn a few precautions. Sometimes the water temperature is a little too refreshing; don't stay in too long, or else hypothermia becomes an issue. Currents are another potential danger, especially during spring runoff and near waterfalls and rapids. As thirsty as you may be, don't ever drink river or lake water. A little organism called *Giardia lamblia* sometimes hangs out in the water, and if it gets inside you, your vacation could be ruined by bloating, fatigue, and far too much time spent on the toilet.

## Yosemite Valley
From mid to late summer, you'll find plenty of swimming holes along the Merced River's sandy beaches at the eastern end of the valley. You can take a dip in Mirror Lake before it dries up the summer, and in Tenaya Creek before fall turns it into Tenaya trickle.

## South Yosemite
The South Fork of the Merced in Wawona is dotted with swimming holes and beaches. There are plenty of lakes in the region's high country, but you have to be an official member of the Polar Bear Club to swim in them. From the Merced Lake High Sierra Camp, you can take a dip in the swimming holes downstream and search for one of our natural waterslides.

It's either a bear in swimming gear or a rare mountain platypus.

## North Yosemite

The Hetch Hetchy Reservoir is a no-go for swimmers, but nearby there's some good summer and fall swimming in a few high country lakes, such as Eleanor, Laurel, and Vernon. Along the Tioga Road the best spot is Tenaya Lake, which has some sandy beaches on its eastern shore. Closer to Tuolumne Meadows, you'll probably need to show your Polar Bear Club membership card again, but there are plenty of places to swim along the river near the Tuolumne Meadows Campground and Lyell Canyon and in some fun lakes such as Elizabeth and Dog.

Just to let you know, none of these spots is a designated public swimming area, so you're in charge of your own safety. Hey, there are always the warm swimming pools at Yosemite Lodge at the Falls and Curry Village—free for paying guests and just $5 per adult and $4 per child for a day for non-guests. Pools are available at the Wawona and Ahwahnee Hotels, but only for overnight guests.

# Where are the best fishing spots?

The fishing here is average—you can fish 127 lakes and reservoirs year-round. If you want my advice, try some of the lakes off Tioga Road such as Lukens, Tenaya, and May Lakes, or some others near the High Sierra Camps. Around Tuolumne Meadows, take your best shot on Cathedral, Elizabeth, and Dog Lakes. Some people like to fish the Hetch Hetchy Reservoir and the rainbow trout fisheries on nearby Laurel and Vernon Lakes.

The fishing season for our rivers and streams runs from the last Saturday in April to November 15. We have a catch-and-release policy here for rainbow trout, requiring barbless hooks, artificial flies, and lures in Yosemite Valley and El Portal. The limit for brown trout is 5 per day or 10 in possession. Fishing from bridges and docks is not allowed nor are live or dead bait fish, amphibians or non-preserved fish eggs. The western end of the valley along the Merced River provides some decent fishing. My favorite stretch is the year-round trout stream (designated "wild") near El Portal. Yosemite Creek and the Dana Fork of the Tuolumne River have been known to yield a fish or two; so has the South Fork of the Merced, where it winds through Wawona.

A valid California fishing license is required for anyone over age 16. You can purchase licenses good for one year for $37.30 for California residents; out-of-staters will be charged $100 at the Sports Shop in Yosemite Village, Curry Village Mountain Shop and the general stores in Crane Flat, Tuolumne Meadows and Wawona. For special regulations in Yosemite Valley, check the *Yosemite Today* newspaper, visitor centers, or park information stations.

# Where can we learn to rock climb?

**W**hen you see the sheer granite cliffs looming large over the valley, you'll wonder how anyone could ever climb these monsters and who would ever want to. Yosemite is actually one of the world's most popular rock climbing areas, attracting hundreds of climbers every year.

You can give the sport a try yourself; the Yosemite Mountaineering School (209/372-8344) is one of the best at teaching the craft of climbing. Classes are offered in Yosemite Valley and in Tuolumne Meadows, weather permitting. They work with families, groups and individuals. Rock climbing takes skill and strength; proper training and conditioning are a must. Whatever you do, don't try scaling our peaks without proper instruction. The rates depend on the number of people in the class and duration of the outing. They cover all skill levels and offer a range of lessons, from a few hours' instruction to snow clibing to two-day big wall seminars.

Watching rock climbers has become a park attraction in its own right. Looking up at the wall of El Capitan or Half Dome, you might see a single tiny speck slowly making its way up the face. It sure isn't me you see up there; it's a person "free soloing" without the help of a climbing partner or rope. It's hard to imagine, but most of Yosemite's largest rock landmarks have been climbed in less than a day.

ROCK CLIMBER

Anyone interested in ...uh... rafting?

121

## Can we go boating on the Merced River?

If you like the idea of floating downstream past breathtaking views of Yosemite Valley, then rafting the Merced is your ticket. In the summer, rental rafts with paddles and life jackets are available at the Curry Village Recreation Center (209/372-4386). Don't worry, you don't have to walk back; a shuttle picks you up and takes you back to Curry Village. The cost is $20.50 per adult and $13.50 for children 12 years or younger (no children under 50 lbs are permitted on rental rafts) for all-day rentals, but it usually only takes 3–4 hours to float the entire stretch between the Yosemite Valley Stables and Cathedral Beach. Due to dangerous rapids in other areas, this is the only section of the Merced open to rafters. Rafts hold 4–6 adults per boat and your rental fee includes paddles and personal floatation devices. Just in case you rock the boat a little too much, it's a good idea to secure valuables in waterproof containers and tie coolers and other items to the raft.

Rafts, canoes, and kayaks can be used on the Merced without a permit. Life preservers, inner tubes, and air mattresses are allowed from Stoneman's Bridge near Curry Village and Sentinel Beach Picnic 10 A.M.–6 P.M. Near Wawona, you can ride the South Fork of the Merced 10 A.M.–6 P.M. from Swinging Bridge to the Wawona Campground. Spring–midsummer, the heavy runoff swells the rivers and streams; that's when it's required to use U.S. Coast Guard- flotation devices. When it gets too dangerous, they close the Merced to all boating and swimming.

The thrill of white-water rafting can be experienced on a 16-mile guided river trip that tackles the rapids around the lower Merced River Canyon outside the park near El Portal. The cost ranges $115–155 per person (including lunch). For more information, contact Mariah Wilderness Expeditions (800/462-7424, www.mariahwe.com).

You can sail and float the waters of eight lakes in the park, but Tenaya Lake is the only one that's easily accessible. You'll have to lug your boat along wilderness trails to reach Merced, May, Benson, Tilden, Twin, Kibbie, and Thousand Islands Lakes. Motorboats are not allowed, and U.S. Coast Guard-approved flotation devices are required for each person on board.

High in the saddle, you can get a unique perspective without ever breaking a sweat while riding the trails in the High Sierra.

Yosemite Valley Stables offers a two-hour guided ride to Mirror Lake, a half-day ride out to the Vernal Fall Bridge area and an all-day ride to the base of Quarter Dome. (This ride is long and strenuous—best left to riders in good physical shape.)

The Wawona Stables offer summer guided rides on the historic wagon road over Chowchilla Mountain and around the Wawona meadow and golf course (two hours) and a ride climbing to the Chilanuala Falls with great views (five hours).

From Tuolumne Stables, there are two-hour rides to Tuolumne View on the Young Lakes Trail, four-hour rides to Tuolumne Falls, and all-day rides covering 18 miles to Water Wheel Falls or a destination suggested by participants.

Children must be at least seven years old and 44 inches tall to ride. Maximum weight is 225 pounds. You can learn about costs and make reservations through DNC (559/253-5636 or 209/372-4386).

If you are interested in traveling to the High Camps you can sign up for four-day and six-day saddle trips—call the High Sierra Desk (559/253-5674) about custom saddle trips.

You can also arrange to bring your own horse to Yosemite, where most of the designated trails are open to stock. Off-trail riding is prohibited, and regulations are pretty tight on animals brought into the park. Privately owned horses, mules, and burros can be kept overnight in the Wawona, Bridalveil Creek, Yosemite Creek, Tuolumne Meadows, and Hetch Hetchy campgrounds, or in the two park stables, by advance reservation and permit only.

> We packed our in-line skates and our skateboards. Is it okay to use them?

I've seen people breezing along the bike paths and paved roads on those in-line skates; it looks like a pretty fun way to get around. You just have to be extra careful of hikers and bikers using the same paths.

Skateboarders looking for good hills to cruise down will be out of luck in Yosemite Valley: It's pretty flat, and it's not a good place to practice all those fancy tricks, like hopping over a deer or a tour kiosk. There are no regulations that say you can't use skates or skateboards in the park, but that will quickly change if rangers see any speed skaters or daredevils bothering other park visitors.

# Can we play golf in Yosemite?

Golfers do have a place to go in Yosemite, and that doesn't mean teeing off the top of Half Dome for a longest-drive contest. The Wawona Hotel (209/375-6572) has a 9-hole, 35-par golf course built in 1918 (open daily, spring–fall) measuring 3,050 yards with lots of challenging roughs and water hazards. This is the only golf course in a National Park! The first hole often has a few deer obstacles that you have to watch out for as well.

The Yosemite golf course is one of the few organic golf courses in the Untied States and is a certified Audubon Cooperative Sanctuary. No pesticides are applied to the course and only reclaimed gray water is used for watering the greens.

If golfing is not your thing, you can still take advantage of the scenic walk through the course's forests and meadows before it opens or after it closes.

You can rent golf clubs and carts at the Wawona Golf Shop, and I recommend reserving a tee time. Prices are $18.50 for 9 holes and $29.50 for a round of 18. Carts will cost you $15 for 9 holes and $24.50 for the long haul. The Wawona Hotel also has an Autumn Golf Package. Contact the hotel for information and reservations, or to learn about lessons.

SHOO!! SHOO!

GRRRRR

Never get between a bear and her clubs!

## Yosemite Valley in the Future

The New Years flood of 1997 began a natural process of change in Yosemite—it damaged rooms, campsites, and picnic areas for visitors, and housing for those who work in the park. In summary, it sped up the process of reducing the impact of visitation on Yosemite Valley.

Now, what nature has started, the National Park Service will carry out in the form of a plan, based on provisions in the 1980 General Management Plan (GMP) to remove unnecessary structures and restore recovered land to a more natural state; to relocate campsites and other facilities out of sensitive or hazardous areas; and to reconfigure roads and build boardwalks to help reduce traffic congestion and visitor impact on the park's ecosystem.

In November 1997, the National Park Service issued their draft Yosemite Valley Implementation Plan (VIP), which outlined four alternatives, each with varying degrees of change and time frames. Then in August 2000, the Environmental Impact Plan was completed for the Merced River Plan followed by the completion of the Yosemite Valley Plan in December. These plans will mean new environmentally sustainable ways for visitors to experience the valley and get around in it in the future. Sixty to seventy percent of this work has already been done, with work continuing on a more limited scale in the future.

A future trip to Yosemite Valley might include some of the following elements:

- Consolidated parking areas and increased energy-efficient shuttle services
- New raised boardwalk pathway systems for bicycle and foot traffic
- Upgraded visitor facilities with improved information, orientation, and way-finding services for visitors

- Interpretive exhibits will be expanded and/or upgraded, with possible human and natural history museums in the valley.
- A new Native American Cultural Center for ceremonial use might be built.
- New amphitheaters will provide space for expanded interpretive programs for campers.
- 147 acres of developed or impacted areas will be restored to a more natural state and other areas will be redesigned to improve visitor circulation or resource management of sensitive or hazardous areas.
- There would be a slight reduction in campsites and lodging accommodations in the valley.

Requests for updates, newletters, and more information on present and future plans for Yosemite Valley should be addressed to:

Yosemite National Park
Yosemite Planning
P.O. Box 577
Yosemite National Park, CA 95389
209/379-1365
yose_planning@nps.gov
www.nps.gov/planning/yose

## Ranger's Farewell

I hope I've answered all of your questions about Yosemite, and I hope that you've learned some inside information on ways to make your visit to the park more enjoyable.

The next part of this book is called the *Quick Reference* section. It's filled with lots of easy-to-find facts, forms, and information about the park. The subjects are in alphabetical order so you can quickly find what you need without having to thumb through the whole handbook. My favorite part of the section is the telephone directory, which gives you numbers for everything I talked about in the book.

Good hunting, and be sure to let us know if we need to change anything to improve future versions of this handbook. You can write to:

Susan Frank or Ranger Dick Ewart
c/o Avalon Travel
1700 Fourth Street
Berkeley, CA 94710
www.avalontravelbooks.com
atpinfo@avalonpub.com

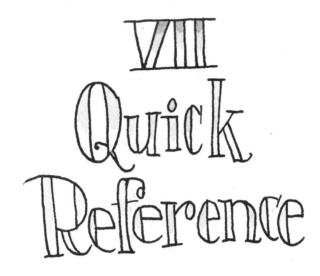

# VIII
# Quick Reference

# CHRONOLOGY OF YOSEMITE'S HISTORIC EVENTS

**1833**    Yosemite Valley was first seen by Euro-Americans. While crossing the Sierra Nevada, the Joseph Walker party encountered a valley with "precipices more than a mile high" which were "impossible for a man to descend."

**1851**    The Mariposa Battalion under the command of Major James Savage became the first group of pioneers to enter Yosemite Valley. They were pursuing "intransigent" Indians.

**1852**    The Mariposa Grove of Giant Sequoias was discovered by a party of prospectors.

**1855**    The first tourist party visited Yosemite Valley with James Mason Hutchings as guide. Thomas Ayres, an artist with the group, made the first known sketches of Yosemite Valley.

**1856**    The first permanent structure, the Lower Hotel, was built in Yosemite Valley at the base of Sentinel Rock. The first trail into Yosemite Valley was completed by Milton and Houston Mann.

**1859**    The first photograph in Yosemite Valley was made by C.L. Weed. His subject was the Upper Hotel.

**1864**    Yosemite Valley and the Mariposa Big Trees were set aside by the federal government as the first state park in the world. Florence Hutchings was the first white child to be born in Yosemite Valley.

**1866**    Galen Clark was named the first Yosemite Guardian.

**1868**    John Muir made his first trip to Yosemite.

**1871**    The first ascent of Mt. Lyell, Yosemite's highest peak, was accomplished by J.B. Tileston on August 29.

**1874**    The first road into Yosemite Valley, the Coulterville Road, was completed. The Big Oak Flat Road was finished a month later.

**1875**    George Anderson made the first ascent of Half Dome before the installation of ropes or cables. The first public school was opened in Yosemite Valley.

**1876**    John Muir's first article on the devastation of the Sierra Nevada by sheep was published.

| 1878 | The first public campgrounds were opened in Yosemite Valley by A. Harris near the site of the present-day Ahwahnee Hotel. |
|------|--------|
| 1890 | Yosemite National Park established. The park did not include Yosemite Valley or the Mariposa Big Trees, but encompassed a large region around them. |
| 1891 | The first telephones were installed in Yosemite Valley. |
| 1892 | Trout were first planted in Yosemite waters by the California Fish and Game Commission. |
| 1896 | Firearms were prohibited from the park. |
| 1898 | The first civilian park ranger, Archie Leonard, was employed at Yosemite. |
| 1900 | The first automobile (a Locomobile) was driven into Yosemite by Oliver Lippincott and Edward C. Russell. |
| 1907 | The first railway line to Yosemite, the Yosemite Valley Railroad, began operation. |
| 1913 | Automobiles were "officially" admitted to Yosemite. |
| 1915 | First appropriation for the construction of the John Muir Trail approved. |
| 1916 | The National Park Service (NPS) was established. Washington B. Lewis was named the first NPS Superintendent of Yosemite. |
| 1917 | The first High Sierra Camp, Tuolumne Meadows Lodge, was installed. |
| 1919 | The first airplane, piloted by Lt. J.S. Krull, landed in Yosemite Valley on May 27. |
| 1921 | The first installations in the Yosemite Museum were completed. |
| 1928 | The Yosemite Museum opened to the public. |
| 1934 | The first water from the Hetch Hetchy Reservoir flowed into San Francisco Bay. |
| 1935 | Badger Pass Ski Area was developed. |
| 1940 | Ostrander Ski Hut was opened for winter use. |
| 1948 | The first ascent of the Lost Arrow Spire by four climbers was accomplished on September 2. |

**1949** The first use of a helicopter for rescue purposes was made at Benson Lake to fly an injured boy to safety.

**1951** The first planting of trout by airplane was done in Yosemite.

**1954** Park visitation exceeded the one million level for the first time in history; 1,008,031 visitors were recorded.

**1958** The first climb up the face of El Capitan was completed.

**1961** Pioneer Yosemite History Center opened to the public.

**1966** New Yosemite Valley Visitor Center built.

**1967** For the first time over two million visitors were recorded.

**1969** The "fire fall" from Glacier Point was discontinued. The famed "Wawona Tunnel Tree" toppled over from the weight of its winter snow load.

**1970** The free shuttle bus system was initiated in Yosemite Valley.

**1972** The first asphalt was removed from the parking lot in front of the Yosemite Valley Visitor Center. The area was converted to use as a pedestrian mall.

**1974** Hang gliding was officially allowed from Glacier Point; 170 flights were made.

**1976** The Tioga Road opened April 10, its earliest opening on record.

**1980** The Yosemite General Management Plan was completed and approved. It was the first systematically developed, long-range planning document for the park.

**1981** Captive-born Peregrine falcon chicks were successfully reared in a nest on El Capitan.

**1983** The first ever prescribed burn was accomplished in the Mariposa Grove of Big Trees.

**1984** Yosemite was named to the World Heritage List. The California Wilderness Bill designated 89 percent of the park as wilderness.

**1986** California bighorn sheep were reintroduced into Yosemite.

**1987** Park visitation exceeded three million for the first time: 3,266,342 visitors were recorded.

**1990** Yosemite celebrated its 100th birthday as a national park. Major forest fires raked the park during August.

**1993**    The Yosemite Concession Services Corp. (YCS) takes over from Yosemite Park & Curry Co. as concessionaire for the park's hotels and business operations.

**1995**    Park visitation exceeded four million for the first time: 4,101,928 visitors were recorded. The first woman to head a major national park, B.J. Griffin, was named superintendent of Yosemite in February. Beginning in March, the park was plagued with rockslides, flooding, and snowstorms that closed roads into the park. Overcrowding and traffic congestion in the summer caused the valley to be closed to cars for seven consecutive weekends. A government budget crunch shut down the park twice over Christmas and New Year's.

**1997**    The worst flooding to hit Yosemite Valley in more than a century closed the park January 1–March 14 and caused extensive damage to roads, utilities, housing, lodging, picnic areas, and campgrounds in the valley. The Yosemite Valley Stable was closed at the end of the summer season, and the draft Yosemite Valley Implementation Plan was issued for public comment. One of the primary goals of the plan is to reduce future crowding and traffic congestion in the valley as outlined in the 1980 General Management Plan.

**2000**    In August, the Environmental Impact Report for the Merced River Plan was completed, and in December, the Environmental Impact Statement was completed for the Yosemite Valley Plan.

**2005**    In April, the Lower Yosemite Fall project was completed. This consisted of a new one-mile walking trail and a new replacement parking area to help reduce traffic and visitor impact on the park's ecosystem. This was accomplished through a public/private partnership at a cost of $13.5 million. In addition, all park shuttle buses were replaced with hybrid buses to help reduce emissions in the park, which made Yosemite the only National Park in the United States to operate all hybrid buses.

**2006**    In October, Olmstead Point Lookout was completely renovated, including new trails and exhibits.

**2007**    The Ahwahnee Hotel celebrated its 80th anniversary. It had been completed in 1927.

Chronology from *The Complete Guide to Yosemite National Park* by Steven P. Medley. Used with the permission of the Yosemite Association.

# EDUCATIONAL PROGRAMS AND EXHIBITS

## Field Seminars

The Yosemite Field Seminar Program sponsored by the Yosemite Association (YA) offers classes geared to educate visitors of all experience levels on a wide range of topics, including botany, geology, ecology, ornithology, Native American culture, art, and photography. They even have family camping trips!

There are outdoor seminars that last 1–6 days. These are usually limited to groups of 10–15 people, and are offered in all areas of the park February–November (weather permitting).

Most of the seminars' prices include shared tent campsites, instruction and part entrance fees. Campers need to bring their own tent, ground cloth, sleeping pad, sleeping bag, flashlight, cooking stove and fuel, food, and all personal gear. All campgrounds have cold running water and flush toilets, but no showers, electricity, or hook-ups. No pets are allowed.

For more information and a listing of current field seminars, contact the YA office (209/379-2321, www.yosemite.org). You can download a PDF of their catalog from the website. Prices depend on length of the trip. If you are a YA member, you qualify for a 15 percent discount.

## Interpretive Programs

Many types of interpretive programs covering a wide range of subjects are offered both day and night in the park. Included are art classes, films, theater productions, and special ranger walks and talks about photography, geology, and the history of Yosemite. Yosemite Valley offers the widest range of programs, but you can also attend a ranger-guided talk at the following locations: Wawona, the Mariposa Grove, Glacier Point, Tuolumne Meadows, Crane Flat, and Big Oak Flat. Check the *Yosemite Today* newspaper for schedule and details.

DNC offers a wide range of fee-based programs including live theater, campfire programs, fireside storytelling, vintage songs and stargazing. Check out *Yosemite Today* for listings, sign up at any Tour and Activity Desk, call 209/372-4386 or visit www.yosemitepark.org.

## Teacher Workshops and Classroom Programs

Since 1971 The National Park Service (NPS), in partnership with the Yosemite Institute (www.yni.org), conducts residential environmental education programs for K-12 schools and other groups. The programs investigate geology, life science, ecology and human history and are aligned with state learning requirements.

Yosemite has a "Parks as Classrooms" program that offers one to two hour ranger-led field trips around the park. The materials presented correlate to the California State Frameworks and include a NPS message of protection and preservation. Spring classes focus on bears; fall classes focus on local Native American culture. Visit the program's website for more information and to learn how to apply for an educational fee waiver to cover your entry fee into the park (www.nps.gov/yose/forteachers/pac.htm).

## Online Information Services

You can browse through several different Yosemite websites for park information and educational programs.

The official NPS Home Page (www.nps.gov/yose) gives you all of the latest information about the park. You'll be able to look through a growing collection of *Yosemite Today* newspapers in PDF format that cover a large variety of Yosemite activities.

The Yosemite Association site (www.yosemite.org) gives you visitor information, a bookstore, a listing of outdoor classes, daily weather forecasts, live webcams of the park, online journal of natural history news in the park and membership information.

The Yosemite Fund site (www.yosemitefund.org) has project updates and funding needs, travel tips, links, videos, and Hikes of the Month along with current donation information.

The DNC website (www.yosemitepark.com) is a great resource for information on lodging, shopping, dining, and park activities.

## Programs at LeConte Memorial

The LeConte Memorial Lodge (209/372-4542, shuttle shop #12), Yosemite's first public visitor center, is run by the Sierra Club and offers a variety of evening environmental education programs geared for visitors, with special children's programs in the summer. Inside you'll find a children's corner, library, and exhibits. It's open 10 A.M.–4 P.M. in the summer. Check out your *Yosemite Today* or call for more information.

## Yosemite Educational Exhibits

American Indian Cultural Exhibit (shuttle stops #5 and #9) displays the cultural history of the native Miwok and Paiute people 1850–present. Open daily from 9 A.M.–5 P.M.

The Yosemite Museum Gallery (shuttle stops #5 and #9) reveals the park as seen through the eyes of many great artists. Check gallery doors or *Yosemite Today* for hours of operation.

The Valley Wilderness Center (shuttle stops #5 and #9) provides essential information and tools for trip planning, minimum-impact camping techniques, and wilderness issues. Open daily from 8 A.M.–5 P.M.

Happy Isles Nature Center (shuttle stop #16) includes natural history exhibits, interactive displays and a bookstore. Open daily from 10 A.M.–4 P.M.

Pioneer Yosemite History Center (Wawona) offers self-guided tours of the Living History exhibit of historic Yosemite buildings, complete with volunteers dressed in period costume. Open summers only.

Mariposa Grove Museum (Mariposa Grove) has exhibits about the amazing giant sequoias. Open summers only.

Thomas Hill Art Studio (Wawona Hotel) presents tours of the artist's studio, where he worked from 1885–1908. Open summers only.

Tuolumne Meadows Visitor Center at Tuolumne Meadows is just south of Tioga Road and west of the gas station. Exhibits explain the Tuolumne Meadows region and Yosemite high country. Open summers only.

# FAMILY ATTRACTIONS

The Yosemite Association has some great books for kids who want to explore the park—you can pick them up at the Valley Bookstore:

***The Happy Camper Handbook*** tells kids (and adults) all they need to know about camping while teaching safety, responsibility, and the outdoors (includes a flashlight and rescue whistle) for $15.95.

The ***Junior Ranger Handbook*** for kids ages 7–13 is sold for $3.50 plus tax at the Yosemite Valley Visitor Center, Nature Center at Happy Isles (May–September), the Tuolumne Meadows Visitor Center (June–September), and Wawona and Big Oak Flat Information Stations (May–September). In order to earn a Junior Ranger patch, the booklet must be completed, a bag of trash collected, and a guided program attended.

The ***Little Cub Handbook*** for kids ages 3–6 is a self-guided booklet that encourages our young visitors and their families to discover Yosemite's wonders and to earn a Little Cubs button. This booklet (published by the Yosemite Association) is sold for $3 plus tax in the Nature Center at Happy Isles, Yosemite Valley and Tuolumne Meadows Visitor Centers, and Wawona and Big Oak Flat Information Stations.

The **Nature Center at Happy Isles** (209/372-0287, shuttle stop #16), geared towards kids, has animal dioramas (great one about nocturnal animals), hands-on exhibits about plants, trees and rocks in Yosemite and a great bookstore. The Nature Center is open daily late spring–October 10 A.M.–4 P.M.

Visit the **Village of the Ahwahnee** located behind the Valley Visitor Center. It's a reconstructed Miwok-Paiute American Indian Village open spring–fall, with a self-guided walking tour. In summer you can see daily "living history" demonstrations of food preparation and hand crafts.

Step back in time at the **Pioneer Yosemite History Center** (209/375-9501, open summer) near the Wawona Hotel. Park rangers and volunteers dress in period costume and give visitors a "living history" of the people and events that shaped Yosemite. Attractions include exhibits and rides in horse-drawn carriages, a working blacksmith shop, and the 126-year-old restored covered bridge that once stood over the Merced River. Self-guided or ranger-led tours are also available.

The **LeConte Memorial Children's Center** (209/372-4542) offers special educational programs for kids during the summer. Check out the *Yosemite Today* for information.

**Daily nature walks led by rangers** take visitors on easy 1–2 hour hikes. Check with any visitor center or the *Yosemite Today* for details.

**Wee Wild Ones,** a ranger-led program for kids ages six and under, has activities and stories at the Curry Village Amphitheater. Check your *Yosemite Today* for times.

**Evening campfire programs and performances** are scheduled at various locations around the park from late June–early September, providing a memorable and entertaining way for families to spend their Yosemite vacations. Check the *Yosemite Today* for times and locations.

**Free art and photography classes** are offered to adults and children ages 10 and older, spring–fall, and during the Thanksgiving and Christmas holidays in Yosemite Valley. Reservations are accepted 24 hours in advance at the Art Activity Center, located at the east end of the Village Mall.

Year-round outdoor recreational activities abound for families. Whether you prefer walking, hiking, biking, horseback riding, rafting, sailing, skiing, snowboarding, snowshoeing, ice skating, or just playing in the snow, you can find it all in Yosemite. Refer to the *Recreational Opportunities* chapter for more information and details.

# HISTORIC PEOPLE AND PLACES

## HISTORIC YOSEMITE PEOPLE

### John Muir

John Muir is probably the most important individual in the history of Yosemite National Park. When the young Scotsman arrived in San Francisco in 1868, he asked directions to "anywhere that's wild." A few years later he was living in a self-built cabin on the banks of Yosemite Creek. Muir worked in Yosemite as a millworker and shepherd, but as he watched more and more settlers and visitors pour into the park and saw how they treated the landscape, he decided his most important job was to protect and preserve the land he came to love. For the remainder of his days, Muir traveled extensively through the Sierra Nevada, studying, documenting, and mapping the terrain. He became a well-known Yosemite guide for many people, including Ralph Waldo Emerson and President Theodore Roosevelt. In 1889, Muir joined forces with magazine editor Robert Underwood Johnson, and together they lobbied for federal protection of the region. Their efforts were rewarded in 1890, when Congress set aside 1,500 acres as Yosemite National Park. Muir later became the first president of the Sierra Club, formed to secure additional preservation and protection for the Yosemite region. Muir died in 1914 at the age of 76.

### Chief Tenaya

When the first Euro-Americans came to Yosemite in 1851, Tenaya was the leader of the native Yosemite people. Revered as a legendary warrior and leader, Tenaya confronted the gold miners who were scouring the region for riches. He told them the Yosemite people would remain peaceful as long as their lives in Yosemite remained undisturbed. Confrontations soon erupted, and in the spring of 1851, a volunteer army called the Mariposa Battalion stormed into the valley to drive Tenaya's tribe out of Yosemite. Tenaya was among a group rounded up and taken to a reservation in Fresno, but he soon escaped to his home in Yosemite. Battles between white settlers and the native people continued, and Tenaya fled with his band to Mono Lake to stay among their allies, the Paiute. In the summer of 1853, Chief Tenaya once again returned to the valley, but he was killed later that same year. A canyon, a lake, and other park features immortalize his name.

### Galen Clark

For 21 years, Galen Clark worked to create and preserve Yosemite National Park. He is known as the pioneer of the homesteading movement in the Sierra

Nevada, where in 1856 he established 160 acres called Clark Station, predecessor of the Wawona Hotel. Clark successfully lobbied to get the Yosemite grant passed and signed by President Abraham Lincoln in 1864, making a small part of Yosemite a state park. For his tireless efforts, Clark was appointed "Guardian of Yosemite," a role he honored by helping to protect the valley and sequoia groves and keeping roads and bridges in good repair to preserve access to the park. Clark died in 1910 just before his 96th birthday; he is buried in the Yosemite Valley Pioneer Cemetery under the sequoias he planted.

## David and Jenny Curry

The Currys were pioneer innkeepers in Yosemite. In 1899 they established a small camp of seven tents and a dining area at the eastern end of the valley. During their first year of business, 292 people registered at the rustic resort, marking the beginning of Camp Curry and its famous tradition of campfire shows and talks in Yosemite. David Curry died in 1917, but "Mother" Curry lived until 1948, long enough to see her camp grow to include lodging for 1,300 guests. In 1925, the Curry Camping Company and the Yosemite National Park Company merged to form a single concession known as the Yosemite Park & Curry Company, which until 1993 operated all concessions in the park.

## HISTORIC YOSEMITE PLACES

**Ahwahnee Hotel** (shuttle stop #3). Before the present hotel was opened in 1927, this was the site of an active stable business known as Kenneyville, which included horses, shops, barns, and houses. When automobile travel became popular, the stable was moved to its present location, and the old buildings were torn down. Between 1943–1945, the Ahwahnee was converted to a Navy convalescent hospital that served almost 7,000 patients.

 **Bridalveil Meadow** (Southside Drive near Pohono Bridge). This is where the Mariposa Battalion, the first Euro-Americans to ever enter Yosemite Valley, camped in 1851. It is here that they proposed the name "Yosemite." President Teddy Roosevelt and John Muir camped here in 1903 to discuss the need to preserve Yosemite's wilderness areas.

 **The Famous Firefall** (Glacier Point). It is believed that the idea for the first firefall came from James McCauley in 1871 or 1872. As a way of attracting visitors to the valley, burning embers were pushed over the edge of Glacier Point to create a stream of fire flowing down the cliff face. David Curry revitalized the tradition in 1899 during his tenure in the valley. Because of the growing negative impact of the event on Yosemite—including meadows trampled by the thousands of nightly spectators, not to mention the traffic jams—the decision was made on January 25, 1968, to discontinue the firefall.

**Pioneer Cemetery** (shuttle stop #3). From the 1870s to the 1950s, residents of Yosemite were buried in the cemetery located across the street from the Yosemite Museum in Yosemite Village. Walking through the cemetery, you'll see the graves of local native peoples Lucy and Sally Ann Castagnetto and of pioneer settlers and innkeepers, such as Galen Clark and James Mason Hutchings. Cemetery brochure guides are available at the Valley Visitor Center.

**Sentinel Rock View** (about 1.4 miles past El Capitan view). This was the site of Leidig's Hotel, which operated from 1869–1888; the site of Camp Ahwahnee from 1908–1915; and later, James McCauley's tollhouse, a collection booth for hikers and horseback riders as they started on the Four-Mile Trail to Glacier Point.

**Stoneman Meadow.** On this site the State of California built a wooden hotel called the Stoneman House, which burned down in 1896. James Lamon, the first permanent pioneer resident of the valley, also built a cabin near here and planted two apple orchards. One of the orchard sites is now the Curry Village parking lot; the other is behind the stables in Yosemite Valley. Stoneman Meadow was also the site of a riot that took place in 1970, when young people clashed with staff over curfews, noise, and lifestyles.

**Yosemite Falls** (shuttle stop #6 for the lower falls, stop #7 for the upper falls). Along the most eastern bank of Yosemite Creek, James Mason Hutchings built a lumber mill to help upgrade his hotel. John Muir ran the sawmill for Hutchings and constructed a cabin nearby for himself. Camp Yosemite, known as Camp Lost Arrow, stood near the base of the fall from 1901–1915.

**Yosemite Lodge** (shuttle stop #8). First built as Army headquarters for the park in 1906, the "lodge" included two large barracks, two bathhouses with lavatories, 156 tent frames, and a parade ground. The army left in 1914; in 1915 the facilities were converted for civilian visitors.

# MEMBERSHIPS AND CONTRIBUTIONS

## The Yosemite Association

The Yosemite Association (YA) is a non-profit organization dedicated to the support of Yosemite National Park through a program of visitor services, publications, and membership activities. It receives no public funds or private endowments. Since 1990, YA has contributed $5.5 million to the National Park Service in Yosemite!

Since 1923, the Association has provided the National Park Service with important financial assistance for research, scientific investigation, education, student intern programs, vehicle donations and environmental projects. Among its programs are the Art Activity Center, the Yosemite Theater interpretive programs, the Field Seminar program, the Ostrander Lake Ski Hut, and the Wilderness Center in Yosemite Valley.

You can go online to to fill out a membership application—your new membership will be confirmed with a return email message and your packet of information will arrive within four weeks. Memberships make great gifts as well—find out more on the Yosemite Association website (www.yosemite.org).

You may also call to become a member (209/379-2317, 8:30 A.M.–4:30 P.M. Monday–Friday). Have your credit card handy.

Levels of membership include:

• Regular Member: $35

• Joint/Family Members: $40

• Supporting Member: $60

• Contributing Member: $125

• Sustaining Member: $250

• Patron Member: $500

• Benefactor Member: $1,000

• International Member: $50

# The Yosemite Fund

Yosemite's popularity, combined with severely limited funding, has taken a huge toll on park resources.

The Yosemite Fund was created in 1988 to provide funding for projects of lasting benefit to Yosemite National Park.

More than 24,000 Friends of Yosemite now share a belief that it is our responsibility to assist in further preserving this one-of-a-kind park.

Friends of Yosemite has supported over 200 projects totaling over $40 million in support:

- Rehabilitation of historic buildings in the Pioneer History Center, Wawona Covered Bridge, the Mariposa Grove, Yosemite Museum and Indian Village
- Acquisition of Native American artifacts, rare books and restoration of early paintings, photographs and films
- Construction and installation of over 2,000 bear-proof storage lockers
- Bringing back the bighorn sheep and peregrine falcon
- Restoring Stoneman Meadow
- Planting hundreds of oak seedlings and willow trees in Yosemite Valley
- Further protecting giant sequoia trees
- Providing wheelchair access to visitor centers and vista points
- And many other projects of significant, long-term benefit to Yosemite

You can make a tax-deductible contribution to help out with projects in Yosemite. Go online to donate electronically (www.yosmitefund.org) or mail your donation to:

The Yosemite Fund
155 Montgomery Street, Suite 1104
San Francisco, CA 94104

- Friends of Yosemite members receive benefits with donations of $25 or more.
- Sequoia Society members make monthly gifts automatically through their credit card or direct debit from their checking accounts.
- John Muir Heritage Society members give $1,000 or more with significant benefits.
- Planned gifts through an estate, trust or will are made possible with the LeConte Society-Planned gifts program.
- Honor and Memorial gifts help honor a loved one.
- You can also make gifts of stock directly to the Yosemite Fund.

Give them a call at 800/4MY-PARK or email info@yosemitefund.org with questions.

# PLACE NAMES OF YOSEMITE

**Ahwahnee:** The Ahwahnechee people's name for both a large village near Yosemite Falls and for the greater Yosemite Valley. Lafayette Bunnell reported that the name meant deep, grassy valley, although this is unsubstantiated. Some linguists believe that "place of a gaping mouth" is a closer translation.

**Big Oak Flat:** A small town near Yosemite's northwestern boundary from which the Highway 120 route took its name. The massive oak (reportedly 10 feet in diameter) which inspired the name is long since dead, the victim of miners' axes in the 1800s.

**Chilnualna:** This name, common in the Wawona area, is of unknown origin and meaning.

**Clark:** Yosemite Valley's first guardian in 1864 and the discoverer of the Mariposa Grove of Big Trees was Galen Clark. His name now graces a mountain, a mountain range, and other features in Yosemite.

**Conness:** A senator from California in the 1860s, John Conness introduced the bill in Congress that set aside Yosemite Valley and the Mariposa Big Trees as a state preserve. Mount Conness is an imposing peak on the park boundary north of Tioga Pass.

**Crane Flat:** Most probably named for a group of sandhill cranes encountered there by Lafayette Bunnell (John Muir also noted cranes at the location.), although some assert the origin was a man named Crane who at one time resided at the spot.

**Curry:** David and Jennie "Mother" Curry established a small tent camp for the public in Yosemite Valley in 1899. It grew to become Camp Curry and later Curry Village. The merger of their operation with the Yosemite Park Company resulted in the Yosemite Park & Curry Co., a long-time concessionaire.

**Dana:** J. D. Whitney's California Geological Survey named a prominent peak east of Tuolumne Meadows for James Dwight Dana in 1863. Dana was a Yale professor and considered the foremost American geologist of his time.

**El Capitan:** This massive granite cliff was named by the Mariposa Battalion in 1851. It is the Spanish equivalent of the native Indian name Too-tok-ah-noo-lah, meaning "rock chief" or "captain." Other names assigned the rock at one time or another were Crane Mountain and Giant's Tower (Go Giants!).

**El Portal:** This Spanish term for gateway or entrance was used to name the terminus of the Yosemite Valley Railroad on the park's western doorstep. Now a small town on Highway 140, the site is slated to become the park's headquarters. Because of its searing summer heat, some have dubbed the place "Hell Portal."

**Glen Aulin:** At the behest of R. B. Marshall of the U.S. Geological Survey, James McCormick named this idyllic spot on the Tuolumne River in the early 1900s with the Gaelic phrase meaning "beautiful valley" or "glen." A High Sierra Camp was built there in 1927.

**Half Dome:** Credit the Mariposa Battalion with describing this split mountain as a half dome. Of all the landmarks in Yosemite, Half Dome has worn the most names over the years, among them Rock of Ages, North Dome, South Dome, Sentinel Dome, Tis-sa-ack, Cleft Rock, Goddess of Liberty, Mt. Abraham Lincoln, and Spirit of the Valley. Somehow a T-shirt imprinted with the phrase "I climbed on top of the Goddess of Liberty" wouldn't quite work.

**Happy Isles:** One of Yosemite Valley's early guardians named the three small islets on the Merced River for the emotions he enjoyed while exploring them ("No one can visit them without for the while forgetting the grinding strife of his world and being happy."). For years this was the site of a fish hatchery.

**Hetch Hetchy:** At one time a remarkably beautiful companion valley to Yosemite, Hetch Hetchy bears a Native American name of several meanings or interpretations, the most popular of which is a kind of grass or plant with edible seeds which abounded in the valley. Some believe *hetchy* means "tree," and that *hetch hetchy* is descriptive of two yellow pine trees that grew at the entrance to the place. Hetch Hetchy was dammed by the City of San Francisco in the 1920s.

**Illilouette:** This French-sounding name is actually an English translation (poor indeed!) of the Native American word *too-lool-a-we-ack.* James Mason Hutchings opined that its meaning is "the place beyond which was the great rendezvous of the Yosemite Indians for hunting deer" (the great Miwok hunt club in the sky?).

**Lembert:** John Baptist Lembert was an early settler in the Tuolumne Meadows region. He built a cabin at the soda springs in Tuolumne, and his name is attached to the granite dome nearby.

**Lyell:** Yosemite's highest peak (13,114 feet) was named by the California Geological Survey in 1863 for Sir Charles Lyell, an eminent English geologist.

**Mariposa:** This Spanish word meaning "butterfly" was first applied to a land grant, later to the community, and then to the county. The sequoias at the south end of Yosemite were called the Mariposa Grove of Big Trees because Galen Clark discovered them in Mariposa County in 1857.

**Merced:** The Moraga party gave the Spanish name to this river when they crossed it in the San Joaquin Valley in 1806, five days after the feast day of Our Lady of Mercy. Originating in Yosemite's high country, the river was formally known as El Rio de Nuestra Señora de la Merced (River of Our Lady of Mercy). All other names utilizing Merced in Yosemite are derived from the river's name.

**Mono:** Derived from the Yokuts people's word *monoi* or *monai,* meaning "flies." At what is now known as Mono Lake, the resident natives harvested, ate, and traded millions of the pupae of flies, a favorite foodstuff of the native people of the region. The Shoshonean tribe grew to be known as the Mona or Mono tribe; many landmarks east of Yosemite bear this name.

**Nevada:** A name assigned to the waterfall on the Merced River by the Mariposa Battalion in 1851. The word signifies "snow" in Spanish; members of the battalion felt that the name was appropriate because the fall was so close to the Sierra Nevada and because the white, foaming water was reminiscent of a vast avalanche of snow.

**Olmsted:** A turnout from the Tioga Road near Tenaya Lake with a remarkable view, named for both Frederick Law Olmsted and his son, Frederick Law Olmsted, Jr. The senior Olmsted was involved in the earliest development of the 1864 Yosemite grant and served as chairman of the first Board of Yosemite Valley Commissioners. His son worked as an National Park Service planner in Yosemite and had a position on the Yosemite Advisory Board.

**Sierra Nevada:** This is the Spanish phrase for "snowy mountain range." It was applied to California's greatest range of mountains by Father Pedro Font, who glimpsed it from near Antioch in 1776. Because the word *sierra* implies a series of mountains, it is both grammatically and politically incorrect to use the term "Sierras." If you do, you will be castigated by self-righteous Yosemite word snobs.

**Stoneman:** A large hotel built by the State of California in 1885 once stood in the meadow just north of Curry Village. Known as the Stoneman House for then-Governor George Stoneman, it burned in 1896. The meadow and nearby bridge still bear the name.

**Tenaya:** The chief of the resident American Indian tribe when the Mariposa Battalion entered Yosemite Valley in 1851 was named *Ten-ie-ya.* The battalion first encountered the Native Americans living near the banks of a lake near Tuolumne Meadows, which they called Tenaya Lake.

**Tioga:** This is an Iroquois word meaning "where it forks," "swift current," or "gate." Miners at work on the Sierra Crest near Yosemite established the Tioga Mining District in 1878, apparently importing the name from Pennsylvania or New York.

**Tuolumne:** An Native American group residing in the Sierra foothills near Knights Ferry was known as Taulamne, reportedly pronounced *tu-ah-lum´-ne.* The name was applied to the river originating in Yosemite and flowing through their territory. The pronunciation of the word in use today is *tu-ah'-lum-e.*

**Vogelsang:** Colonel Benson, an American officer and acting superintendent of Yosemite National Park 1905–1908, named a peak south of Tuolumne Meadows for either Alexander Vogelsang or his brother Charles Vogelsang, both of whom were affiliated with the California Department of Fish and Game. *Vogelsang* is German for "birdsong," an apt name for the site of the Vogelsang High Sierra Camp.

**Wawona:** Popular opinion holds that the word is the Native American name for "big tree." Native peoples viewed the big trees as sacred and called them *who-wo-nah.* The word is formed in imitation of the hooting of an owl that they believed to be the guardian spirit and deity of the sequoias.

**White Wolf:** A meadow on the route of the Tioga Road named by John Meyer who, while chasing the Indians came to the temporary camp of White Wolf, the band's chief.

**Yosemite:** This name was assigned to the world's most beautiful valley by the Mariposa Battalion in 1851. They believed that the Yosemite people (as they were apparently known) who resided there should have their true name perpetuated in the designation of the valley. The exact meaning of the name is disputed, but Lafayette Burnell, a member of the battalion, later wrote that the term signified "grizzly bear." He was informed that because grizzly bears frequented the territory occupied by the Yosemites and because the band was skilled at killing the bears, the name was taken as an appropriate one for the people.

Yosemite Place Names from *The Complete Guide to Yosemite National Park* by Steven P. Medley. Used with the permission of the Yosemite Association.

# PRESERVATION PROJECTS IN YOSEMITE

In September of 1980, the National Park Service (NPS) issued a General Management Plan for Yosemite National Park (GMP) with the stated goals of restoring and preserving nature, as well as reducing traffic. In 1992, the plan was amended by the Concession Services Management Plan and Final Environmental Impact Statement. Another plan in 2000, called the Yosemite Valley Plan, aimed to help carry out the five broad goals outlined in the GMP. Then in 2004, the User Capacity Management Program for the Merced River Corridor described management tools used by the BPS to address visitor use within the Merced River corridor. Here are some of the projects in progress or completed to meet those goals:

## Habitat Conservation and Restoration Programs

Along the bikeway between Yosemite Village and Yosemite Falls, plastic tubes protect black oak seedlings within roped-off areas. The goal is the restoration of a black oak woodland damaged by people and overgrown with conifers that competed with the oaks for space and light.

Some of the pioneer settlers and early park managers placed boulders and barriers in the Merced River, changing its flow. The National Park Service now has a restoration program designed to return the Merced and its ecosystem to a more natural state and has instigated a new catch-and-release regulation in Yosemite Valley to protect native rainbow trout.

Several of Yosemite's meadows are in the process of being restored. Volunteers have planted native vegetation, fenced meadows, installed boardwalks to channel foot traffic, and removed invasive non-native plant species.

When hikers step around muddy trails, they actually create new trails. In some meadows, four or more trails are cut, side by side. The NPS, with the help of the California Conservation Corps and other volunteers, has been filling and replanting the ruts in these trails, building raised causeways, and protecting the natural integrity of the meadows. Visitors can help by staying on established trails.

The 1995 High Sierra Camp season was canceled due to environmental concerns after a very wet winter. To reduce stress on the backcountry trails, Yosemite Concession Services and NPS initiated a High Sierra trail conservation program, which includes eliminating the transport of over 21 tons of specialty produce and linen into the backcountry each season. You'll still be able to eat generous portions of prepared meals at the High Sierra Camps, but without the heavier fruits and vegetables. You might want to bring your own 13.4-ounce travel sheet, since bed sheets are no longer provided.

Fire is an essential element in Yosemite's ecosystem. It reduces dead and down fuels, thins old vegetation, recycles nutrients, and enhances the health of our plants, many of which depend on fire for survival. Under certain safety conditions, the prescribed burning program uses controlled fires in areas of the park during early summer and mid-fall. Since 1970, prescribed burns have restored 32,000 acres within the park; a little extra smoke in the air is worth it in the long run. For the same reason, in 83 percent of the park's wilderness, lightning-caused fires may be allowed to burn without intervention in areas full of dead and down fuel and where there's no threat to property or human lives.

To increase protection of river habitat and riparian resources, the Merced River has new rafting regulations. Rafters are asked to disembark only on sand or gravel bars. Fallen trees are no longer removed from the river, since they provide fish habitats and add nutrients to the aquatic food chain. The river will be closed when the water level is too high (seven feet or higher at Sentinel Bridge) or too low, when floating activities might disturb the river-bottom habitat.

## Protection of Endangered Species and Animal Reintroduction Programs

Peregrine falcons are making a comeback in Yosemite after being absent for many years. The NPS and the Santa Cruz Predatory Bird Research Group, with funding help from organizations and individuals, have helped increase the number of peregrines. Four nesting pairs with eight young were counted in 1995.

California bighorn sheep once roamed the Yosemite area, but they were eradicated by hunting, disease, and competition for food. Today the NPS, U.S. Forest Service, and California Department of Fish and Game have helped return the bighorns to the park's eastern edge. There are continuing studies to protect these animals from external threats such as disease from domestic sheep grazing near park boundaries.

## Wildlife Studies

Mountain lions, peregrine falcons, goshawks, great gray owls, black bears, bats, and amphibians are being studied by the NPS in an effort to ensure their survival.

## Reduction of Traffic and Pollution

The YCS maintains a fleet of shuttle buses, including emission-free electric-diesel hybrid models, that shuttle visitors between 22 points of interest in the valley. If the electric buses significantly help to reduce emissions in the valley, more will be added to the fleet until all park shuttles are powered by electricity or other alternative fuel sources.

## Recycling in Yosemite

Yosemite has one of the most extensive recycling programs in the national park system. Started in 1975, the program has won several national and state awards.

Glass, aluminum, paper, cardboard, and some plastics are accepted at the park's recycling centers at the Village Store and Curry Village. Refunds are also given for soft drink and beer containers at stores where the drinks are purchased.

Green recycling receptacles are located throughout park campgrounds, at picnic areas, and at many roadside turnouts.

Since 1988, there haven't been foam cups or containers in the park, due to the fact that they are non-biodegradable and a waste of costly fuels. Most of the hotel paper products and printed materials are made from recycled paper. Freon used in both park refrigeration systems and auto batteries is recycled.

## Partners in Preserving the Park

The Yosemite Fund is a San Francisco-based, non-profit charitable organization that raises funds for preservation and restoration projects in the park. Since 1988, the fund has provided more than $40 million for more than 200 Yosemite improvement programs. You can help efforts to preserve and restore Yosemite by ordering a distinctive four-color Yosemite Valley license plate. The plate is issued by the DMV for vehicles registered in California. For more information, contact the Yosemite Fund (800/4MY-PARK, 415/469-7275, www.yosemitefund.org).

Along with the Yosemite Fund, many active partners help raise money, sponsor educational programs, publish park information, and donate time and materials. These include the Yosemite Association, Yosemite Institute, Sierra Club, Ansel Adams Gallery, San Francisco Conservation Corps, National Park Foundation, and Sousson Foundation, to name a few.

There are also scores of individuals who donate time and money, some of whom spend their vacation time working on park projects. These volunteers clean up rivers and trails, rehabilitate campgrounds, revegetate meadows and woodlands, uproot non-native plants, and act as campground hosts. You can join Yosemite's partners by joining the Yosemite Fund, the Sierra Club, or the Yosemite Association service project, or by volunteering for the NPS Volunteers in the Parks (VIP) Program.

# TELEPHONE AND WEBSITE DIRECTORY

## GENERAL INFORMATION

**DNC Parks & Resorts at Yosemite**
559/253-5636 (accommodation reservations)
www.yosemitepark.com

**National Park Service**
209/372-0200
www.nps.gov/yose

**Yosemite Fund**
415/469-7275 or 800/4MY-PARK
www.yosemitefund.org

**Yosemite Association**
209/379-2317
www.yosemite.org

## GETTING THERE

**AMTRAK**
800/872-7245
www.amtrak.com

**California Parlor Car of San Francisco**
415/474-7500
www.calpartours.com

**DNC Parks & Resorts at Yosemite**
559/253-5636 (accommodation reservations)
www.yosemitepark.com

**Gray Line**
888/428-6917
www.grayline.com

**National Park Service**
209/372-0200 (recorded general park information),
800/436-7275 (camping reservations)
www.nps.gov/yose

**Preferred Charters**
707/585-9110

**Road conditions**
209/372-0200
www.nps.gov/yose/planyourvisit/conditions.htm

**Tower Tours**
866/345-8687
www.towertours.com

**VIA Adventures**
209/384-1315 or 800/VIA-LINE
www.via-adventures.com

**YARTS**
877/989-2787
www.yarts.com

**Yosemite Fee Office**
209/372-0207
www.nps.gov/yose/planyourvisit/waivers.htm

*Yosemite Today*
www.nps.gov/yose/planyourvisit/today.htm

## KENNELS
**The Animal Care Center**
209/742-7387

**Doggone Gorgeous**
209/962-4688

**Graydon Kennels**
559/683-8836

**Hoof N Paw**
559/683-3313

**Ritter Animal Hospital**
209/966-5666

**Yosemite Valley Stables**
209/372-8348

## PARK ATTRACTIONS
**Ansel Adams Gallery**
209/372-4413
www.anseladams.com

**Badger Pass Ski School**
209/372-8444

**Big Trees Tram Tour**
209/372-4386

**Glacier Point Tour**
559/252-4848

**High Country Saddle Tour**
559/253-5674

**Self-Guided Tours**
www.nps.gov/yose/planyourvisit/brochures.htm

**Tuolumne Meadows Visitor Center (ranger-led walks)**
209/372-0263

**Wawona Information Station (ranger-led walks)**
209/375-9501

**Yosemite Grand Tour**
209/372-4386
www.yosemitepark.com/Activities_GuidedBusTours.aspx

**Yosemite Mountaineering School (guided high country walks)**
209/372-8344
www.yosemitepark.com/Activities_HikingCamping_
OvernightBackpackingTrips.aspx

**Yosemite Valley Tram Tours**
209/372-1240

# LODGING AND DINING
## Lodging inside the Park
**DNC Parks & Resorts at Yosemite**
559/253-5636
www.yosemitepark.com/Reservations.aspx

**Evergreen Lodge**
209/379-2606
www.evergreenlodge.com

**Meadows Lodge**
559/253-5635

**The Redwoods in Yosemite**
209/375-6666
www.redwoodsinyosemite.com

**White Wolf Lodge**
559/253-5635

**Yosemite West Reservations**
559/642-2211

# Lodging outside the Park

**Apple Tree Inn**
559/683-5111
www.appletreeinn-yosemite.com

**Best Western Yosemite Way Station**
209/966-7545
www.yosemiteresorts.us

**Buck Meadows Lodge**
209/962-5281

**Cedar Lodge**
888/742-4371
www.yosemiteresorts.us

**Lakeview Lodge**
760/647-6543 or 800/990-6614
www.lakeviewlodgeyosemite.com

**Mariposa Lodge**
800/966-8819
www.mariposalodge.com

**Marriott's Tenaya Lodge**
888/514-2167
www.tenayalodge.com

**Mother Lode Lodge**
209/966-2521
www.mariposamotel.com

**Narrow Gauge Inn**
888/644-9050
www.narrowgaugeinn.com

**Oakhurst Lodge**
888/431-9907
oklodge@sti.net

**Shilo Inn**
559/683-3555
www.shiloinns.com

**Yosemite Gateway Best Western**
559/683-2378
www.yosemitegatewayinn.com

**Yosemite Gateway Motel**
760/647-6467
www.yosemitegatewaymotel.com

**Yosemite View Lodge**
209/379-2681 or 888/742-4371

**Yosemite Westgate Lodge**
800/253-9673
www.yosemitewestgate.com

## Dining inside the Park
**Ahwahnee Dining Room**
209/372-1489

**Evergreen Lodge**
209/379-2606

**Mountain Room (Yosemite Lodge at the Falls)**
209/372-1274

**Tioga Pass Resort**
760/647-6423

**Tuolumne Meadows Lodge**
559/252-4848

**Wawona Hotel Dining Room**
559/253-5686

**White Wolf Lodge**
559/252-4848

## Dining outside the Park
**Buck Meadows Lodge**
209/962-5281

**Castillo's Mexican Food**
209/742-4413

**Cedar Lodge Bar & Restaurant**
209/379-2316

**Charles Street Dinner House**
209/966-2366

**Coffee Express**
209/962-7393

**The Groveland Hotel**
209/962-4000

**Happy Burger**
209/966-2719

**Hotel Charlotte**
209/962-6455

**Jackalope's Bar and Grill at the Tenaya Lodge**
559/683-6555

**The Mono Inn**
760/647-6581

**The Narrow Gauge Inn**
559/683-6446

**Nicely's Restaurant**
760/647-6477

**Savoury's Restaurant**
209/966-7677

**Sierra Restaurant at the Tenaya Lodge**
888/514-2167

**Tioga Gas Mart and Whoa Nellie Deli**
760/647-1088

**Yosemite View Restaurant & Lounge**
209/379-2681

## Seasonal Events
**Bracebridge Dinner at the Ahwanee**
559/253-5604

**Special events packages**
559/253-5636
www.yosemitepark.com/SpecialEventsPackages_EventEvents.aspx

# CAMPING AND BACKPACKING
**High Sierra camps**
559/253-5674
www.yosemitepark.com/Accomodations_HighSierraCamps.aspx

**National Park Service**
209/372-0200
www.nps.gov/yose

National Park Service and
National Forest Service campground reservations
877/444-6777
www.recreation.gov

**Trail conditions**
www.nps.gov/archive/yose/wilderness/trailconditions.htm

**Wilderness permits**
209/372-0200
www.nps.gov/yose/wilderness

**Yosemite Association Field Seminar Program**
www.yosemite.org/seminars/index.html

**Yosemite Association store**
www.yosemitestore.com (bear-proof canisters)

**Yosemite Mountaineering School**
209/372-8344

# RECREATIONAL OPPORTUNITIES
## Bicycling
**Bike rental (Yosemite Lodge)**
209/372-1208

**Curry Village Recreation Center**
209/372-8319

## Boating
**Curry Village Recreation Center**
209/372-4386

**Mariah Wilderness Expeditions**
800/462-7424
www.mariahwe.com

## Golf
**Wawona Hotel**
209/375-6572

## Horseback Riding
**DNC Parks & Resorts at Yosemite**
559/253-5636 or 209/372-4386

**High Sierra saddle trips**
559/253-5674

## Rock Climbing
**Yosemite Mountaineering School**
209/372-8344

## Winter Activities
**Badger Pass**
209/372-8430
www.yosemitepark.com/BadgerPass.aspx

**Ice skating**
209/372-8319

**Motor coach tour**
209/372-4386
www.yosemitepark.com/Activities_GuidedBusTours.aspx

**Yosemite Mountaineering School and Guide Service**
209/372-8444

**Yosemite Tubing Area**
209/372-8444

## EDUCATIONAL PROGRAMS
**DNC Parks & Resorts at Yosemite**
209/372-4386
www.yosemitepark.org

**Educational fee waivers**
www.nps.gov/yose/forteachers/pac.htm

**LeConte Memorial Lodge**
209/372-4542

**Yosemite Association**
209/379-2321
www.yosemite.org

**Yosemite Institute**
www.yni.org

## FAMILY ATTRACTIONS
**LeConte Memorial Children's Center**
209/372-4542

**The Nature Center at Happy Isles**
209/372-0287

**Pioneer Yosemite History Center**
209/375-9501

# MEMBERSHIPS AND CONTRIBUTIONS
**Yosemite Association**
209/379-2317
www.yosemite.org

**Yosemite Fund**
415/469-7275 or 800/4MY-PARK
www.yosmitefund.org

# PRESERVATION PROJECTS
**Yosemite Fund**
415/469-7275 or 800/4MY-PARK
www.yosemitefund.org

# VISITOR SERVICES
**Yosemite Accessibility Guide**
www.nps.gov/yose/access

# WHERE CAN I FIND...?
**DNC personnel office**
209/372-1236
www.yosemitepark.com

**Lost & Found**
209/379-1001 (NPS), 209/372-4357 (DNC)

**NPS human resources office**
209/379-1805

**Village Garage**
209/372-8320

**Volunteering**
www.nps.gov/yose/supportyourpark/volunteer.htm

**Yosemite Bookstore**
209/379-2648

**Yosemite Institute program office**
209/379-9511

**Yosemite Lodge Bellman's Room**
209/372-1274

**Yosemite Medical Clinic**
209/372-4637

# VISITOR SERVICES

## Materials and services for international visitors:

The "One Day In Yosemite" video in the Valley Visitor Center and the Yosemite Valley Audio Guide are both available in four foreign languages: French, German, Spanish, and Japanese. Many of the brochures about Yosemite are in the same four languages, and the Yosemite Association sells translated picture guides. Some park employees can act as translators, but only in emergencies.

## Facilities and services for visitors with physical disabilities:

Golden Access Passes are available for visitors with disabilities, allowing lifetime admission and discount pass for blind or permanently disabled U.S. citizens or permanent residents. Passes are available at entrance stations or visitor centers.

For visitors with mobility disabilities—if a visitor does not have a handi-cap placard, a temporary placard can be obtained at visitor centers. This permits driving access on the Happy Isles Loop and to Mirror Lake/Meadow. One must drive 10–15 mph and have flashers on. Visitors unable to board the Mariposa Grove Tram may drive behind a tram and have a cassette tape tour of the grove (spring–fall). Visitors with temporary disabilities are not entitled to the Golden Access Passport, but can receive temporary placards that per-mit use of disability parking spots.

The Yosemite Accessibility Guide is available at park entrance stations, visitor center, and online (www.nps.gov/yose/access). TTY's are available inside The Ahwahnee Hotel and Yosemite Lodge, and outside the Valley Visitor Center and Curry Village front desk.

Accessible parking spaces are available just west of the Yosemite Valley Visitor Center. To reach these, enter the valley on Southside Drive and go west (left) to Sentinel Drive. Turn left on Northside Drive, and follow the blue-and-white accessibility signs.

All buildings in the park have handicap access. Most of the valley camp-grounds and four of the valley hikes are accessible with assistance. Check the *Yosemite Today* for details.

Many of the visitor activities, like the art classes, ranger-guided walks, and the photo and John Muir walks, are wheelchair accessible. Check the *Yosemite Today* for details.

The Yosemite Medical Clinic (8 A.M.–5 P.M. Monday–Friday, and 9 A.M.–noon on Saturday) rents wheelchairs for $10/day.

During the summer, the National Park Service employs at least one sign language interpreter. Visitors who would like to request that the interpreter be available at an activity may contact the sign language interpreter through the rangers in the visitor center. The "One Day In Yosemite" video and film shown in the Valley Visitor Center are both captioned. Yosemite Theater programs may be interpreted by advance arrangement.

## Special services and discounts for older persons:

All U.S. Citizens and legal residents ages 62 and older can purchase a Senior Pass for a one-time fee of $10 from any of the park entrance stations. These passes provide discounts at all specified park facilities and tours.

# WHERE CAN I FIND...?

### Where can I find a gas station?

Year-round stations are located in Wawona in the south part of the park via Highway 41 south towards Fresno (25 miles from the valley), El Portal via Highway 140 west towards Mariposa (14 miles from the valley) and in Crane Flat in the north portion of the park. Tuolumne Meadows also has a station via 120 east towards Nevada (54 miles from the valley), but it is open only in the summer.

### Where can I find a towing and repair service for my car?

The Village Garage (209/372-8320, daily 8 A.M.–5 P.M.) is available for towing, repairs and service. They sell propane until 4 P.M. and have 24-hour towing.

### Where can I buy propane or diesel fuel?

You can buy propane in the valley at the Village Garage, El Portal or at Wawona year-round and at Tuolumne Meadows in the summer. Diesel fuel can be purchased at El Portal outside the valley (24 hour, pay-at-the-pump with credit or debit card), Crane Flat, and Wawona.

### Where can I find Internet access?

Internet access is available to park visitors at three locations: Yosemite Lodge (24 hours, $5.95 for half-day, $9.95 for full-day, $25 for three days, or use a kiosk for $0.25 a minute), Degnan's Café (7 A.M.–5 P.M. for a fee), and the Mariposa County Library south of the Yosemite Cemetary (free during limited hours Monday–Thursday).

### Where can I get cell phone service?

Digital cell service is available in and near Yosemite Village to AT&T and Verizon customers. (You may get a weak signal elsewhere in Yosemite Valley, as well.) Verizon customers with analog-capable phones may receive service near Wawona, Crane Flat, and Tuolumne Meadows.

### Where can I find medical care?

The Yosemite Medical Clinic (209/372-4637) is located on Ahwahnee Drive in Yosemite Valley. The clinic provides routine and emergency medical care, 24-hour paramedic and ambulance service, limited pharmacy, lab, x-ray, and physical therapy.

## Where can I find public restrooms? A public shower? A public laundromat? Storage lockers?

Public restrooms are open at the following locations in the valley: near the parking lot for Yosemite Falls, across the street from Yosemite Lodge; behind the Valley Visitor Center; near the parking lot at the east end of Yosemite Village; at the Happy Isles Nature Center; near the Glacier Point parking lot; and at various locations along the backcountry trails.

You'll find public showers at Curry Village (all year) and seasonal showers with restricted hours at White Wolf Lodge, Housekeeping Camp and Tuolumne Meadows Lodge. Remember, there are no public showers in Wawona. There's a laundromat at the Housekeeping Camp. You'll find coin-operated public lockers at Curry Village on the west side of the registration office. The Yosemite Lodge Bellman's Room (209/372-1274) will often take an item for the day only.

## Where can I find a post office? An ATM machine?

The park's main post office is open year-round in Yosemite Village. There's also a small year-round post office at Yosemite Lodge and the Wawona Store. ATM machines are available in Yosemite Village south of and inside the Village Store, inside the main registration area at the Yosemite Lodge, inside the gift/grocery story in Curry Village, and on Highway 140 at the Yosemite View Lodge and the El Portal Market.

## Where can I cash a check, get a cash advance, or have foreign currency exchanged?

You can cash a personal check at the cashier's office located just beyond the Village Store with the following stipulations: picture ID and major credit card or check guarantee required; no two-party checks; $5 fee; $100 limit per day.

Guests of park lodging facilities may cash checks at front desks. You may cash one check for $50 or less per day without being charged a fee. Cash advances against credit cards (Visa, Mastercard, and Discover) are handled on a prorated fee basis. Foreign currency exchanges are not available in the park.

## Where can I find the Lost & Found office?

NPS and YCS each have separate Lost & Found offices. Visitors reporting a lost item should complete a Lost & Found Report at both a NPS visitor center or information station and at a DNC lodging front desk. Contact NPS Lost & Found (209/379-1001) or DNC Lost & Found (209/372-4357).

## Where can I find a photocopy machine? Send or receive a fax?

You can find a photocopy machine at the Yosemite Lodge, the Ahwahnee Hotel, and Curry Village. A fax can be sent and received through the front desks of the Yosemite Lodge, Curry Village, and the Ahwahnee Hotel.

## Where can I get an America the Beautiful or Senior Pass?

The America the Beautiful—Annual Pass (good for all National Parks and Federal Recreation Lands for one year from date of purchase) can only be purchased from rangers at park entrance stations. The cost is $80 annually. A pass valid only for Yosemite will cost $20 for one week and $40 for one year. Senior Passes, which are lifetime passes to all National Parks, can also only be purchased at park entrance stations and now require a one-time fee of $10 when issued to qualifying senior citizens (U.S. citizens or legal residents ages 62 or older).

## Where can I get a job in Yosemite? Where can I volunteer to work in the park?

The National Park Service (NPS) has long lead-times for hiring. Contact the human resources office (209/379-1805). The Delaware North Companies (DNC) also has a personnel office located in the DNC General Office Building located at the opposite end of the Yosemite Village Mall from the Valley Visitor Center. Apply in person at the office (209/372-1236, 9 A.M.–5 P.M., Mon.–Fri., www.yosemitepark.com) or download an application from their website.

There are a number of ways to be a volunteer in Yosemite National Park through the NPS—campground host, biological technician, information specialist, fire prevention and more. For more information visit www.nps.gov/yose/supportyourpark/volunteer.htm.

## Where can I find the Superintendent's office? The Chief Ranger's office?

To contact the Superintendent's Office, write to: Superintendent, P.O. Box 577, Yosemite, CA, 95389. The Superintendent's office is located on the ground floor of the Administration Building near the Valley Visitor Center. To contact the Chief Ranger, write to: P.O. Box 577, Yosemite, CA 95389. The Chief Ranger's office is located on the second floor of the NPS Valley Administration Building.

## Where can I find the Yosemite Institute office?

The Yosemite Institute (YI) program office (209/379-9511) is the second building to the left of the Yosemite Cemetery. YI's business office is located in El Portal, just west of the El Portal Market.

## Where can I find the U.S. District Court/Magistrate's office?

On Village Drive between the NPS Maintenance Yard and the Post Office. A sign points north to the U.S. District Court.

## Where can I find the jail?

Make sure that you have approved business at the Law Enforcement Office before you go. Exit from the front of the Visitor's Center and immediately turn right down the path that goes past the Yosemite Museum building. Turn right up the road just beyond the Museum, and go up the road to the NPS maintenance yard/parking area. Follow the fire lane to the back of this area and to the large concrete building housing the NPS Firehouse. A door immediately to the right of the large Firehouse garage doors is marked "Law Enforcement Office;" go to the second floor.

# WILDERNESS CAMPERS' & BACKPACKERS' CHECKLIST

## Clothes
- Sturdy hiking boots
- Thick hiking socks
- Lightweight liner socks
- Long underwear
- Fleece pants and sweatshirt
- Rain-resistant jacket and pants
- Warm hat and gloves
- Oversocks and gaiters
- Set of extra clothes
- UV protection sunglasses

## Equipment
- Rain-resistant sleeping bag and pad
- Backpacking tent and stakes
- Frame backpack
- Flashlight/headlamp
- Water bottle
- Backpacking stove and fuel
- Cooking pot, cup, and utensils
- Lighter or waterproof matches
- Compass, map, pocket knife, and watch
- Water purification device
- Lightweight rope for hanging food
- Bear-resistant canisters

## Supplies
- Sunscreen, insect repellent, lip balm
- Small first-aid kit with blister kit
- Toilet items
- Food

## Temperatures and Climate

| | JAN | FEB | MAR | APR | MAY | JUNE | JULY | AUG | SEPT | OCT | NOV | DEC |
|---|---|---|---|---|---|---|---|---|---|---|---|---|
| Rainfall (in.) | 6.2 | 6.1 | 5.2 | 3.0 | 1.3 | 0.7 | 0.4 | 0.3 | 0.9 | 2.1 | 5.5 | 5.6 |
| Max temp °F | 49 | 55 | 59 | 65 | 73 | 82 | 90 | 90 | 87 | 74 | 58 | 48 |
| Min temp °F | 26 | 28 | 31 | 35 | 42 | 48 | 54 | 53 | 47 | 39 | 31 | 26 |

# WILDERNESS PERMIT INSTRUCTIONS

Wilderness permits can be obtained in person at the Wilderness Center in Yosemite Valley or at one of the stations listed below. At least 40 percent of each trailhead quota is available up to one day in advance, on a first-come, first-served basis. If you plan a Saturday start date, have a large group, and/or plan to use popular trailheads such as those in the Tuolumne Meadows area or to Little Yosemite Valley, Half Dome, or Merced Lake. You probably should make a reservation or pick up your permit a day in advance, early in the day, to assure trailhead access. Permits for the trail to Half Dome are only issued at the Yosemite Valley Permit Station, and you can count on a long line each morning.

Send a letter that includes the dates you plan to enter and exit the wilderness, the specific trailheads where you plan to start and end, your principal destination, number of people in your group, and number of stock or pack animals, if appropriate. Be sure to include alternative dates and/or trailheads in case your first choice is not available.

Mail reservation requests to: Wilderness Reservations, Wilderness Center, P.O. Box 545, Yosemite, CA 95389. Be sure to include a $5 processing fee per person, and make your check payable to the Yosemite Association. Requests will be processed 24 weeks in advance of the first day of your trip. Making a request does *not* guarantee a reservation. If your requested trailhead and dates are available, you will receive a confirmation letter in the mail. If your reservation request is made less than two days or more than 24 weeks in advance, it will be rejected *without notice.* You may also reserve by phone or online (209/372-0740, 8:30 A.M.–4:30 P.M. Mon.–Fri., www.nps.gov/archive/yose/wilderness/reserve.htm).

A $5 per person non-refundable processing fee is charged for all confirmed reservations. Payment by check or money order should be made to the Yosemite Association. Credit card payments are accepted with valid card number and expiration date. Reservation phone lines are often busy. We encourage you to make your request in writing. Mailed requests are processed simultaneously with phone requests.

You may also complete the task in person at one of the following locations:

- **Yosemite Valley Wilderness Center** (open summer only; visitor center in winter): Located in Yosemite Village next to the post office.

- **Big Oak Flat** (open summer only; self-registration during winter): Located on the Big Oak Flat Road (Highway 120) at the park entrance.

- **Tuolumne Meadows** (open summer only; self-registration at ski hut): Located in parking lot 0.25 mile from the Tuolumne Meadows Ranger Station.

- **Badger Pass** (open winter only): Ranger Station A-Frame at Badger Pass on Glacier Point Road.

- **Hetch Hetchy:** Hetch Hetchy Entrance Station. The Hetch Hetchy Road is open limited hours. There is no access to Hetch Hetchy trailheads while the road is closed.

- **Wawona** (open summer only; self-registration during winter): Information Station in the Hill's Studio, adjacent to the Wawona Hotel, just off the Wawona Road (Highway 41).

# YOSEMITE MIWOK LEGENDS

## The Legend of Half Dome

In the days of the bird and animal people, one man traveled to Mono Lake to marry Tesaiyac. On their way back to Yosemite, she said she wanted to return to her home. They quarreled, and Tesaiyac started running back to Mono lake. With her husband in pursuit, she flung the basket she was carrying at him, and it became Basket Dome. Then she threw a baby cradle, where the Royal Arches are today. Because anger had been brought into Yosemite, the couple were turned to stone. He became North Dome and she, Half Dome, where you can still see the trail of her tears on the granite face, the same tears that formed Mirror Lake. Some say you can see the image of Tesaiyac in the vertical face of Half Dome.

## The Legend of Tultakana

Long ago, two bear cubs living in the valley went swimming in the river. After they were done, they climbed to the top of a huge boulder to dry in the sun. They fell asleep and slumbered through many moons, and while they slept the boulder rose slowly to the heavens, until their faces scraped against the moon. The bird and animal people tried to bring the cubs down, but all failed. Along came Tultakana, a measuring worm, who was able to inch his way up the boulder and carry the cubs back down. In honor of the rescue, the boulder was named "Tultakana." Today it's known as El Capitan.

## The Legend of U-wu-lin, the Giant of Ah-wah'-nee

When the first bird and animal people inhabited the Valley of Ah-wah'-nee, it was a time of plenty, and they lived well. Then a great cannibal giant, U-wu-lin, appeared in the north and began to eat the people. The bird and animal people tried in every way to kill the giant, but nothing they could do would hurt him. Their arrows glanced from his body, and their spears were broken against his huge sides. The giant's heart was located in a tiny spot in his heel, and it was his only point of weakness. The bird and animal people, however, did not know where to find it. They asked Fly, who had a terrible bite, if he might help.

Fly went out to search for the giant and found him asleep; he began biting the giant everywhere. The giant gave no indication that he was aware of Fly until his heel was bitten; then he kicked his massive leg. Fly then knew he had found the giant's weak spot, and he returned to the bird and animal people to announce his exciting discovery.

The people decided to make a large number of long, sharply pointed stakes, which they placed all along the trail traveled by the giant. When the giant came down the trail, one of the awls pierced the heart in his foot, and he died immediately. In this way, peace was restored to the Valley of Ah-wah'-nee.

Excerpted with permission from *Legends of the Yosemite Miwok,* published by the Yosemite Association, 1993

# · Further Reading ·

Many of the following books may be purchased from the Yosemite Bookstore, which has sales facilities at Visitor Centers throughout the park. Call or write to place your order or to request a publications catalog:

Yosemite Bookstore
P.O. Box 230
El Portal, CA 95318
209/379-2648

- *Birds of Yosemite and the East Slope,* by David Gaines, illustrated by Keith F. Hansen. Lee Vining, California: Artemisia Press, 1992 (revised).

- *Complete Guidebook to Yosemite National Park, The,* by Steven P. Medley. Yosemite National Park: Yosemite Association, 1994.

- *Discovering Sierra Birds,* by Edward C. Beedy and Stephen L. Granholm, illustrated by Keith Hansen, John Petersen, and Tad Theimer. Yosemite Natural History Association and Sequoia Natural History Association, 1985.

- *Discovering Sierra Mammals,* by Russell K. Grater, illustrated by Tom A. Blaue. Yosemite Natural History Association and Sequoia Natural History Association, 1978.

- *Domes, Cliffs, and Waterfalls: A Brief Geology of Yosemite Valley,* by William R. Jones. Yosemite National Park: Yosemite Association, 1990.

- *Draft Yosemite Valley Implementation Plan and Supplemental Environmental Impact Statement,* produced by the United States Department of the Interior, National Park Service, Yosemite National Park, California, 1997.

- *Easy Day Hikes in Yosemite,* by Deborah J. Durkee, illustrated by Michael Elsohn Ross. Yosemite National Park: Yosemite Association, 1985.

- *50 Best Short Hikes in Yosemite and Sequoia/Kings Canyon,* by John Krist. Berkeley, California: Wilderness Press, 1993.

- *Gilbert Stanley Underwood: His Rustic, Art Deco, and Federal Architecture,* by Joyce Zaitlin, A.I.A. Malibu, California: Pangloss Press, 1989.

- *Handbook of Yosemite National Park,* compiled and edited by Ansel F. Hall. New York and London: G. P. Putnam's Sons, 1921.

- *Legends of the Yosemite Miwok,* compiled by Frank La Pena, Craig D. Bates, and Steven P. Medley, illustrated by Harry Fonseca. Yosemite National Park: Yosemite Association, 1993 (revised).

- *One Hundred Years in Yosemite,* by Carl Parcher Russell. Yosemite National Park: Yosemite Association, 1992.
- *Place Names of the High Sierra,* by Francis Farquhar. San Francisco: Sierra Club, 1926.
- *Sequoias of Yosemite National Park, The,* by H. Thomas Harvey. Yosemite National Park: Yosemite Association, 1978.
- *Wild Heritage: Threatened and Endangered Animals in the Golden State,* by Peter Steinhart. California Department of Fish and Game, California Academy of Sciences, and Sierra Club Books, 1990.
- *Yosemite: A Guide to Yosemite National Park,* produced by the Division of Publications, National Park Service. Washington, D.C.: U.S. Department of the Interior, 1990.
- *Yosemite As We Saw It: A Centennial Collection of Early Writings and Art,* by David Robertson, assisted by Henry Berrey. Yosemite National Park: Yosemite Association, 1990.
- *Yosemite National Park: A Natural History Guide to Yosemite and Its Trails,* by Jeffrey P. Schaffer. Berkeley: Wilderness Press, 1989.
- *Yosemite Place Names,* by Peter Browning. Lafayette, California: Great West Books, 1988.
- *Yosemite Road Guide,* by Richard P. Ditton and Donald E. McHenry. Yosemite National Park: Yosemite Association, 1989 (revised).
- *Yosemite: Saga of a Century,* edited by Jack Gyer. Oakhurst, California: The Sierra Star Press, 1965.
- *Yosemite's Historic Wawona,* by Shirley Sargent. Yosemite, California: Flying Spur Press, 1979.
- *Yosemite's Yesterdays,* by Hank Johnston. Yosemite, California: Flying Spur Press, 1989.
- *Yosemite Trout Fishing Guide,* by Steve Beck. Portland, Oregon: Frank Amato Publications, Inc., 1995.
- *Yosemite Valley: Secret Places & Magic Moments,* by Phil Arnot. San Carlos, California: Wide World Publishing/Tetra, 1992.
- *Yosemite Wildflower Trails,* by Dana C. Morgenson. Yosemite National Park: Yosemite Association, 1975.

# ·Index·

## SUSAN AND PHIL FRANK

Susan Frank spent many of her childhood weekends camping in the Sierra Nevada and fishing California rivers and lakes with her family. She saw her first grizzly bear on the Katmai Peninsula in Alaska at age ten and spent more enjoyable hours waiting for fish to bite her line than actually catching them. After earning a degree in European history from the University of California, Berkeley, she taught in Minnesota and California before starting a career in communications. In 1990, she founded a media and marketing consulting company, working with a variety of clients throughout the San Francisco Bay Area.

Cartoonist Phil Frank's daily cartoon strip *Farley* kept a finger on the pulse of the San Francisco Bay Area for more than 21 years, ever since Phil decided to move the strip from national syndication to focus his considerable talents on issues closer to home. The strip was dearly loved and followed daily by a local cadre of fans. Indeed, *Farley* became one of San Francisco's most recognized and reliable landmarks. In 2004, Phil started a nationally syndicated strip with writer Joe Troise called *Elderberries,* which turned a humorous eye to the issues of aging in America. Phil passed away in September of 2007, but his *Elderberries* strip still runs in newspapers across the country.

Susan and Phil started their life together on a houseboat in Sausalito, California. This led to their first book collaboration, a children's book about living on the water. Both avid history buffs, they moved from ship to shore about 10 years ago. Susan lives in Sausalito in a 1914 Craftsman-style home, from which she ventures into California's national parks and other wilderness areas in search of inspiration for new books. Her family includes two grown children, three grandchildren, and Gus, a feisty Cairn Terrier.